FORD, 1921 - WALKERVILLE

McLAUGHLIN, 1921 - OSHAWA

A GREAT WAY TO GO

A GREAT WAY TO GO

THE AUTOMOBILE IN CANADA

ROBERT COLLINS

THE RYERSON PRESS/TORONTO/WINNIPEG/VANCOUVER

© THE RYERSON PRESS, 1969

SBN 7700 0290 0

For Lesley and Cathy

ACKNOWLEDGMENTS

This book was prepared with the cooperation of members of The Antique and Classic Car Club of Canada.

Grateful acknowledgment is made to the following for the use of illustrations: Alberta Motor Association: page 67 (bottom, left); Hal Arthurs, photographer: page 98 (top); Antique and Classic Car Club of Canada: pages ii, viii, 8, 9, 21 (bottom), 28, 44, 52, 60, 72, (top), 74 (except top), 75, 76 (top), 95, 96, 97, 98, 99, 100, 101, 102, 103 (bottom) 104, 105, 106, 121 (bottom), 122 (bottom), 128 (second from top), 130 (top), 141 (top); Antique Auto Museum, Niagara Falls, Ontario: pages 42 (top), 71 (bottom), 124, 130 (bottom), 141 (bottom), 145; Harold Brillinger, photographer: pages viii, 37, 41 (top and middle), 42 (top), 44, 71 (bottom), 72 (top), 96 (bottom, right), 97, 98 (bottom), 99, 100, 101, 102, 103, 104, (bottom), 124, 130 (top and bottom), 132 (bottom), 141 (bottom), 145; Canadian Good Roads Association: pages 11, 27, 62 (bottom, left), 63 (top), 80 (bottom left and right), 81, 82; Canadian Road Transport Association: page 58 (right); CKEY: page 87; Chrysler-Plymouth, Detroit: page 115 (bottom); U. H. Dandurand Collection: pages 3 (bottom), 5 (top), 61; E. H. Davis: page 128 (top); Department of Highways, Ontario: pages vi, 38, 46, 49 (bottom), 57, 59, 67 (bottom, right), 69, 70, 85, 86, 88 (bottom), 90 91, 119; H. B. Donovan: page 65 (top, right); Gordon Doolittle: pages 7 (bottom), 80 (top), 83, 84, 144 (top); Dupont of Canada, Limited: pages 74 (top), 142 (bottom), 144 (bottom); Ford of Canada, Oakville: pages 45, 47, 49, 54 (middle and bottom), 55, 56, 114, 115 (top), 116, 117, 118; Fort Malden National Historic Park, Amherstburg, Ontario: page 121 (top); R. Garner: pages 128 (bottom), 144 (middle); General Motors of Canada, Limited: pages 29, 30 (left), 31 (bottom), 32, 34, 39 (bottom), 40, 41 (bottom), 43, 113; Glenbow-Alberta Institute: pages 4 (right), 15, 22, 24 (top), 35, 50, 53 (bottom), 54 (top), 58 (left), 63 (bottom), 68, 77, 108, 131 (bottom); *The Globe and Mail*, Toronto: pages 94 (bottom), J. McNeil, photographer; William M. Gray: pages 3 (top), 126 (top), 132 (top); Hans P. Gulde, photographer: page 111; Hamilton Automobile Club: pages 1 (top), 5 (bottom, left and right), 6 (middle and left), 7 (top), 12, 14 (top and bottom), 24 (bottom, left), 65 (bottom, right), 94 (top), 130 (middle); *The Hamilton Spectator:* pages 2 (top and bottom), 6 (bottom); Nelson Holmwood: page 140 (bottom); Imperial Oil, Limited: pages 72 (bottom), 88 (top); Jerry Vogel Music Co. Inc., 121 West 45 St., New York, N.Y. 10036, assigned copyright for "The Little Ford Rambled Right Along," words and music by C. R. Foster and Byron Gay, copyright 1914, renewed 1941, used by permission of copyright owner: page 48 (top); *Kitchener-Waterloo Record:* pages 16, 137 (top); *London Free Press*: page 51; Manitoba Archives: page 76 (bottom); Memory Lane Bookshop: pages 19, 24 (bottom, right), 30 (right); Metropolitan Toronto Library Board: pages 4 (left), 13, 18, 126 (bottom), 127 (top), 134; Metropolitan Toronto Police: pages 53 (top), 65 (bottom, left), 66 (bottom); Moose Jaw Public Library: page 125 (middle); Harley Neilson: page 96; Ontario Motor League: pages vii, 1 (bottom), 10, 20, 21, (top and right), 23, 31 (top), 62 (top and bottom right), 64, 65 (top, left), 66 (top), 67 (top), 71 (top), 123, 125 (top), 128 (second from bottom), 131 (top), 135 (bottom), 137 (bottom), 138 (top), 139 (except bottom), 140 (top), 142 (top); Oshawa Automotive Museum: pages 37, 41 (top and middle), 103 (top), 132 (bottom); *Saskatoon Star-Phoenix*: page 73; N. C. Schneider: page 17; F. David Stone, photographer: page 112; *Toronto Star Syndicate*: page 42 (bottom); Tudhope Specialties Ltd.: page 26; University of Western Ontario, Library: page 138 (middle and bottom); *Winnipeg Free Press*: Page 6 (top).

COLOUR INSERTION Harold Brillinger, photographer; Antique and Classic Car Club of Canada; Antique Auto Museum, Niagara Falls, Canada; Centennial Centre of Science and Technology; Imperial Oil Ltd.; Oshawa Automotive Museum; F. David Stone, photographer (racing pictures); Peter Weatherhead.

Every effort has been made to credit picture sources. The publisher would appreciate information which would correct any errors or omissions.

PRINTED AND BOUND IN CANADA BY THE RYERSON PRESS

CONTENTS

INTRODUCTION	vii
"COME ON BOYS, USE THEM AS DEMONS"	1
"ALWAYS LET UP ON THE SPEEDER..."	16
WHEELS IN HIS HEAD	29
AND THE LITTLE FORD RAMBLED RIGHT ALONG	44
THE CLOAK AND GOGGLE HEROES	57
AN END TO INNOCENCE	69
DR. DOOLITTLE AND THE LONG, LONG ROAD	79
THE BUGS WITH DETACHABLE BRAINS	87
FINE ART ON FOUR WHEELS	95
"YOU NEED A LOT OF GUTS"	107
A DRIVE INTO THE TWENTY-FIRST CENTURY	113
THE CANADIAN CAR DIRECTORY	120
MAJOR UNITED STATES MANUFACTURERS	146
COMMERCIAL VEHICLES	147
THE SAD SHORT LIFE OF THE CALGARY CAR	147
HOW THE HORSELESS GREW AND GREW	148
BIBLIOGRAPHY	149
INDEX	151

INTRODUCTION

Of all the creations of modern man, none so dominates his life as the thing called "automobile." Once a curiosity, then a luxury, it is now deemed an absolute necessity by three-quarters of the people in Canada. Some of us are conceived in it; a few are born in it; many die in it.

For hundreds of thousands, from assembly line worker to the car hop at a drive-in restaurant, it is a living. For millions more the car is a way of getting to work. For other millions it is simply a way of life: pleasure, social indicator, dearest possession, and the second most *costly* possession in most families. It dictates where and how we live. We talk about it more than our jobs, the weather or our children.

Being true self-effacing Canadians we tend to think that America invented the motor car. In fact, Europe had it first and Canadians were tinkering with the horseless carriage as early as any Ford, Duryea or Apperson. Who has heard of the Fossmobile, the Menard, LeRoy, Maxmobile or Bourassa Six? They were all Canadian cars, as were dozens more. All are gone now, except the few collected and lovingly restored by vintage car enthusiasts, but once they were part of Canada's growing up, as were all the events that surrounded them.

This is the story of those cars and the people who made, drove and loved them; how the automobile began, grew, pervades our life today and where it is apt to go from here.

1

"COME ON, BOYS, USE THEM AS DEMONS!"

For one particular band of Ontario picnickers, the world —or at least *their* gentle uncomplicated world—came to an end on a summer Sunday in 1898. They were peaceably chomping their hard-boiled eggs and roast drumsticks when a *thing* burst into the hushed green sanctity of Burlington's LaSalle Park, a spindly buggy-like machine with 36-inch wire-spoke wheels and a curved leather dash. Clearly, this was a buggy gone wrong: indecently nude and even frail-looking without the faithful horse in front.

Yet it was neither frail nor friendly. It surged toward them propelled by some hideous power deep in its innards. High in its buggy seat rode a man with a square craggy face, a blissful glint in his eye and a tiller in his hand.

"It's that Moodie from over Hamilton," somebody said. "It's the horseless he got from Cleveland. I read about it in the *Spectator*."

And John Moodie it was, owner of Canada's second gasoline motor car and the first ever imported (he'd got it past the astonished customs men, and knocked 10 per cent off the duty, by calling it a locomotive). Moodie stopped his new $1,000 Winton runabout and waited for the open-mouthed admiration he'd been getting in Hamilton.

Some of the picnickers *did* flock around, jabbering, pointing, cautiously touching. But then their leader did what any right-thinking man in authority would have done; what men have always done when faced with something new and frightening.

"Get out!" he cried. "This is a private gathering. Get that thing out!"

Moodie pulled away, slowly, with all the noise and majesty that a one-cylinder motor could muster, leaving the picnickers full of awe, foreboding and heartburn. He had just added to his string of "firsts"—the first real head-on

James Moodie, charter member and first secretary of the Hamilton Automobile Club, in his father's Winton about 1900. This is the same model as the car owned by his uncle, John R. Moodie, which was the first car imported into Canada.

Colonel John R. Moodie and his family, about 1902, in their second car—a Winton.

confrontation between a Canadian motorist and his natural enemies, the non-motorists.

Moodie was thoroughly equipped for the encounter. Being forty-six and a wealthy industrialist, he'd been in scraps before and did not scare easily. He was in fact committed to a lifelong quest for the untried and unlikely. He'd been first in the district to have a high-wheeled bicycle, with which he'd won chestsful of medals for racing; first in Hamilton with a player piano; first, many years later in partnership with Timothy Eaton, to bring a turbine steamship across the Atlantic. Those qualities—curiosity and unlimited guts—made him the ideal pioneer motorist.

On April 2, 1898 he bought the second Winton ever made, and missed getting the first by a day. On April 12 he became the first motorist to drive the streets of Hamilton. Months after, on a visit to Toronto, he reportedly caused the first traffic jam—three blocks of gawking pedestrians and panicky horses around Yonge and Melinda streets. A year later he taught Mrs. Moodie how to handle the car, thus inflicting on the startled nation its first woman driver.

He was by no means the first motorist in Canada, but the other pioneers shared his burning desire to experiment, to press on regardless of obstacles. Without it they couldn't have survived. The whole story of their beginning years was grief and frustration, caused either by their wretched unpredictable machines, or by their fellow men whose attitudes ran from indifference to murderous hate.

This "Night Service Buggy" appears to have been home-made in the Hamilton area, about 1902. It was propelled by a one-cylinder chain drive and had a radiator.

With the Rev. Georges Belcourt, parish priest of Rustico, P.E.I., the local reaction was a kind of communal yawn. In 1866 he brought to town a "single-seated steam wagon." The local press, dismissing it with a line, never bothered to find out where or how he got it. When Father Belcourt displayed it at a July outdoor tea party, the Charlottetown *Examiner* reported it was "put in motion and with great wonder and delight was observed steaming away for a half mile on the road and back again, at a fast speed, after which the meeting dispersed with good order, all appearing well pleased with the day's proceedings." But they were not pleased enough to encourage the priest with money or even a vote of thanks. He and the steamer vanished from history.

The next year Henry Seth Taylor, a Stanstead, Que., watchmaker, unveiled before an equally bored public his steam buggy, product of seven years planning and building. It was a four-wheel one-seater open carriage with tiller steering, a water tank over the front axle and a wood-fired boiler with sixty pounds pressure. On its maiden run at the Stanstead fair a hose broke, swallowing Taylor and buggy in clouds of steam. The locals collapsed with laughter.

Taylor dried himself off, repaired the damage and a few days later took a spin out of town. Going over the brow of a hill with the boiler simmering at his back, he remembered an accessory he'd meant to add: brakes. He jumped just before the buggy crashed. A sensitive man, Taylor waited until after dark to haul the pieces back to his loft. Then he got out of the car business.

Thirty years later George Foote Foss, a young bicycle repairman, built a one-cycinder gasoline car and took it out on the streets of Sherbrooke. By now the horseless was known to anyone who read a newspaper. The Duryea brothers, Henry Ford and others were tinkering with vehicles in the United States. Frederick Fetherstonhaugh, a lawyer, had created a stir with his electric car at the 1893 Toronto Fair. However, Sherbrooke viewed Foss's gas buggy as a dangerous weapon. He could coax 12 mph out of it on a good day and that, warned the city fathers, would get him thrown in jail if he kept it up! Foss ignored them and drove the car four more years. The same tactic worked for U. H. Dandurand, who "illegally" drove Montreal's first horseless, a Waltham steamer, and subsequent cars for three years before the city would give him a permit.

It was not merely that the public feared the motor car and didn't *want* to believe in it. Most people simply

An electric posed in front of the Parliament Buildings, Toronto. Chatham's William Gray believes that his father's firm of carriage and sleigh makers may have built the body.

Mr. U. H. Dandurand and family with his Waltham Steamer. It was the first car in Montreal, November 21st., 1899. Note the trailer, also the first to appear.

John Craig Eaton, later Sir John, at the tiller of his "smart electric runabout," in front of the Eaton garage, one of the first "houses for automobiles" to be built in Toronto.

W. F. "Billy" Cochrane, about 1902, in his Locomobile the first automobile to be brought into Alberta.

couldn't take it seriously in a world brimming with other ridiculous inventions and simple pleasures. By 1903 the Wright brothers had made their first tentative flip-flop into the air. A fantastic moving picture device, the nickleodeon, was bringing *The Great Train Robbery* and other delights to the continent. The Boer War was over, the peek-a-boo shirtwaist was coming in and Alberta's Frank Slide had buried a town and killed seventy-six people. Saskatchewan and Alberta would soon become provinces—ah, how great the Dominion was growing! Everybody sang "She's my tootsie wootsie in the good old summertime." Everlasting health for the nation was assured with Dr. William's Pink Pills for Pale People and Dr. Chase's Syrup of Linseed and Turpentine. Who needed that freakish motor car? It wouldn't last. It would *never* replace the horse.

Only the curious, the compulsive searchers and innovaters, believed in it. Among them the motor car craze spread like fever. Soon after Moodie bought his Winton, John Craig Eaton, son of Timothy and later Sir John, got one too. Then Vancouver businessman W. H. Morrison heard about it and in February 1899 sent a partner, W. C. Ditmars, down east to bring one back. Eaton took him for a ride but the Winton stalled six times going around a couple of blocks. Ditmars prowled on into the U.S. and eventually bought a steamer from the not-yet-famous Stanley brothers of Newton, Mass.

Two years later Billy Cochrane of a Calgary ranching family (whose name for decades graced the steepest hill in central Alberta) bought a Locomobile. The Calgary *Albertan* ranked this news item well below reports that Mrs. Ed English was back from Seattle and that Calgary might hire the Salvation Army band to play in its parks.

U. H. Dandurand demonstrating his 1902 De Dion-Bouton, a French gasoline car. It had the first registered plates in Montreal. Mr. Dandurand donated it to the Chateau de Ramezay museum in Montreal, where it still exists today in running condition.

Gradually, though, incredulity was changing to belief, wonder and rage. When George Millen, managing director of the Eddy Match Company, drove his new steamer outside Ottawa in 1900, farmers came running to the roadside, convinced the machine was bewitched. Four years later "Ace" Emmett, Manitoba's pioneer motorist, delivered a one-cylinder Cadillac to Regina. The trip took four days and all along the way curious farmers pressed him with offers of food and overnight lodging. They were *lonely* farmers, though; scattered like pinpoints through a vast empty land still called the Northwest Territories. They'd make friends with anybody, even a rancher. From then on, for a half-dozen years, when farmers came running at automobiles, they were usually behind levelled pitchforks.

Already that spring Emmett had led a Winnipeg delegation to nearby Headingly, offering to build a free road. The local councillors turned him down: "We don't want those new-fangled motor machines scaring our horses off the highway!" Down east, farmers and motorists were close to civil war.

A Hamilton resident, S. O. Greening, and his family out for a drive in their Robinson car, about 1901. Greening was the first president of the Hamilton Automobile Club and owned one of the first garages in Hamilton.

The members of the Winnipeg Automobile Club in 1904, just before setting out on their first country run. A. C. "Ace" Emmett is in the passenger's seat in the first car on the left.

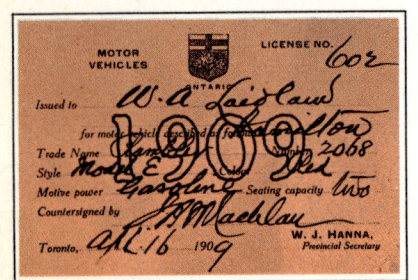

The horseless had a name now, from the Greek *autos* ("self") and the Latin *mobilis* ("moving"), which gave rural people a focal point for their hatred. Everything about the automobile was repugnant to them. It represented violent change, which they resented on principle. It was noisy and stinking. A history of Belleville, Ont., graphically describes the town's first car, a one-cylinder Packard: "A cloud of white smoke and evil-smelling fumes floated in sulphurous haze behind. Housewives opened doors and stood goggle-eyed. Small boys lined the walks and proceeded with measured pace alongside, keeping up easily with the speed. Down Pinnacle Street they proceeded without incident, other than scaring the wits out of a number of weaker-hearted citizens and the daylights out of placid horses that had never before been known to shy even at a thunderstorm."

The farmers alleged that cars also scared pigs, killed chickens, caused cows to dry up and drove their women into

W. A. Laidlaw driving an Oldsmobile about 1908. Mr. Laidlaw was one of the foremost motoring pioneers in the Hamilton area, where he still resides.

On the right is S. O. Greening's Robinson. The feet protruding from under the other car belong to Sir Frank Baillie, who apparently found it necessary to make some on-the-spot repairs.

hysterics. The last was partly true; some Edwardian women were genuinely afraid of the auto although they faced dirt, disease and Canadian winters with total aplomb. When Montrealer L. C. Rivard drove out near Joliette one day, an old woman threw her apron over her head and ran screaming, "*Mon Dieu, le diable est arrivé!*"

Another cause for general alarm was the fact that most drivers knew less about driving than today's pre-schooler knows about piloting a moonship. Horseless drivers still had the instincts of horsemen. An Assiniboia, Sask., farmer was still vainly pulling on his new Ford's steering wheel, like reins, as he plunged through a neighbor's greenhouse. A Kitchener felt manufacturer, Oscar Peterson, was seen careering down a hill, over a boardwalk, through a fence and into a vacant lot, bellowing "WHOA, WHoa, whoaaaa . . ." Ben Trumper of Weyburn received his car by freight, started for his farm home after dark and, having no headlights, asked a friend with a lantern to walk ahead. The car soon outran the lantern bearer and Trumper ran up on a rockpile. Countless others drove into the sides of houses or through the ends of the barns and carriage sheds that served as garages.

A very rare photo of the Still made by the Canadian Motor Syndicate, Toronto. Mr. Gordon Doolittle has four photos of this vehicle, tied together with blue ribbon, that were presented to his father, Doctor Perry E. Doolittle. The hand-lettered caption for this photo is "FIRST CANADIAN MOTOR CARRIAGE standing on grade of 1 in 3 (or 33 ⅓ per cent) by its own motive power. (No brakes whatever had been fitted at the time photo was taken). To make the test more severe, the ground (a soft, sandy loam) was covered with boards where wheels touch."

PREPARING FOR A MOTORING TOUR—1904 (Instructions are those given at the time).

Starting for a two weeks tour. There should not be more than three in the car, as the baggage fills half of the tonneau.

Filling the water tank at the garage before the start. A funnel with a strainer is being used so that no impurities may get into the radiator.

Inexperienced motorists sometimes forget the all-essential gasoline. Roughly speaking, a gallon is good for ten or fifteen miles.

Before packing the luggage, lay everything on the ground to see that nothing called for in the schedule is left behind. The inner tubes, to prevent their being chafed, are to be carried in the rubber bag that rests on the extra tire.

In touring, the covers are carried over the lamps in the daytime. The extra "shoe" is being strapped to the mudguards—one of the ways in which it may be carried.

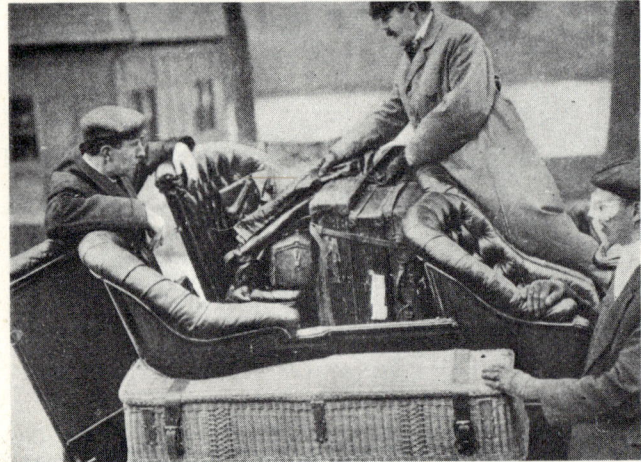

The suit-cases, after being strapped to the seat and side of the car to prevent their being jolted out of place, are covered with a rubber blanket.

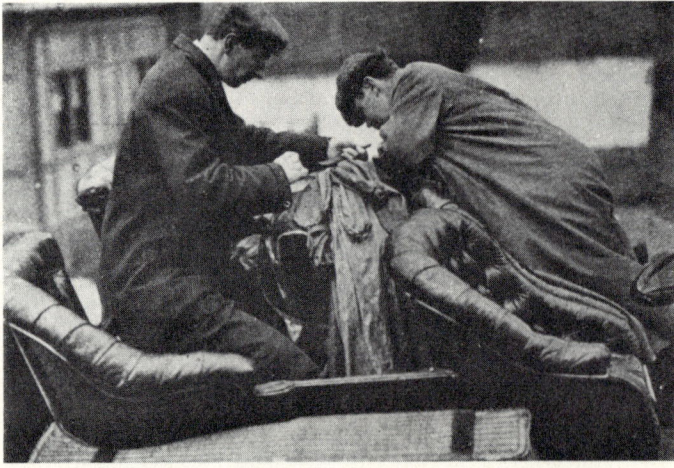

The last step in the packing—the rubber coats are placed on the top of the covered pile of luggage, so that the baggage need not be opened and exposed to the weather when the coats are wanted in an unforeseen rain-storm.

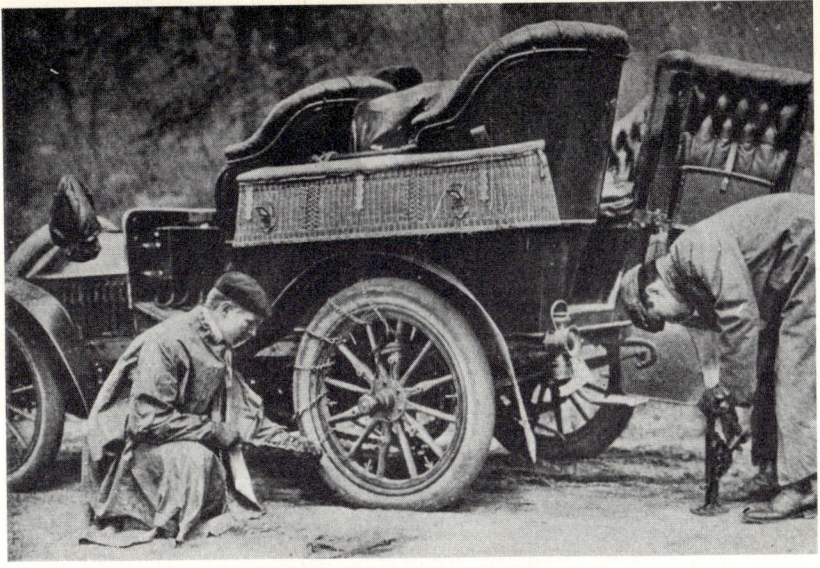

Deep mud ahead—chaining the rear tires for traction. Ends of the chain should be attached to straps that are wound around the spokes.

The canvas dust-shield is a valuable accessory. Note the nail-pulling device on the rear tire, which will generally prevent a nail from piercing the inner tube.

Stopping for the night at a wayside house. The seating portion of the car should be completely covered with rubber blankets.

On a tour in a tonneau, with dust shield in position. The side baskets are rubber-lined and do not need to be covered.

There was no count of traffic accidents, but a prevailing joke reflected the pedestrians' bitter mood: "First Motorist—Does running over a pedestrian upset you? Second—No, I've never run over one that big." Nor were the non-drivers much comforted by the credentials of so-called automobile mechanics. When W. L. Kane imported Nova Scotia's first car from Toronto, it had to be assembled by the local fire department. Most other "mechanics" were blacksmiths.

Faced with this threat to their lives and livelihood, the farmers mobilized. They laid trees, telegraph poles, nail-studded planks, broken bottles, barbed wire and upturned saw blades in the roads. A few stretched thin invisible wire across the trail, level with drivers' necks. Their sons capered by the roadside in knickers or overalls, sailing their caps into the road, enough to make a nervous driver twitch the tiller and veer into the ditch.

A motorist who asked directions got the contemporary catch-line, "Mister, yew can't get there from here!", followed by a rural guffaw. The ultimate humiliation was breaking down or getting stuck and having to ask for a pull. While little children chanted "GET A HORSE!" the farmer uncorked a blistering stream of abuse and a demand for $5.00.

For some, a convenient mudhole or expendable chickens were a form of guaranteed income. There was a farmer who told his neighbor, "I got ten cows for the railroad to run over and lots of hawgs for them auto fellows. Figure I'll clear $500 this summer."

The motorists retaliated, at least once. One Sunday morning five Winnipeggers, including a lawyer and a judge, drove to Poplar Point, where they met five other vigilantes, including the mayor of Portage la Prairie. Hiding in the bushes, they watched a local farmer lovingly prepare a mudhole and camouflage it with straw. They grabbed him

Downtown Toronto, 1906

and offered him the option of trial on the spot or a formal charge in Winnipeg. He chose the instant trial, was "sentenced" to twelve dippings head first in one of his own water barrels, then set to filling the hole with gravel.

But two-thirds of Canada's population was rural, and when farmers spoke politicians listened. They hurt motorists most of all with the law. Ontario led off in 1903 with a 15 mph country and 10 mph town speed limit. Even this was a concession from the proposed 7 mph in urban areas. The Toronto and Hamilton motor clubs had to take each MLA for a ride to persuade him that 10 mph wasn't unduly reckless.

British Columbia enacted the same law in 1904. In Quebec, with an 8 mph limit, drivers had to ring a bell on approaching every intersection. Saskatchewan's first limits, set in 1906, were 10 mph in towns and 20 on the rural roads; drivers had to sound a "proper alarm, bell, gong or horn" to warn pedestrians of their approach. A year later Nova Scotia set a rural speed limit of "one mile in eight minutes."

In every province motorists had to slow down when approaching a horse-drawn vehicle, stop on the driver's signal or if the horse seemed frightened, and if necessary get out and "render assistance." Time after time farmers made cars stop, then drove on snickering. Over and over motorists had to lead balky horses while their ungrateful drivers cursed and raged. When Nelson Good stopped his LeRoy near Galt to lead a horse-drawn wagon, the animal reared and slashed at him, narrowly missed his head and tore his coat from his back. "Smart horse," grunted the farmer.

There were, as well, local bylaws that gave police almost godlike authority. In 1904 C. F. Grundy was arrested for "placing an automobile on Vaughan Street in the city of Winnipeg, which is an obstruction to the safety of travel on said street." At the Calgary Stampede in 1907 a real estate man was jailed for parking his car where it might frighten the horses.

The complacency of the Victorians is readily seen in this stylish turn-out of 1910.

In 1904 these men, wrapped in furs, made a fast trip from Hamilton to St. Catharines in one hour and twenty minutes—quite an accomplishment, particularly in winter.

Even this didn't pacify the farmers. In 1904 the Newcastle, Ont., *Independent* thundered, "Is it not time something was done to put a stop to the automobile business? They are becoming such a curse to the country that we cannot stand it.... These people have no regard for us or our horses and when the latter are frightened they laugh like a quartet of idiots. But with our shotguns and barbed wire the laugh may turn. Come on, boys, and use them as demons, not as human beings!"

One county council petitioned the Ontario legislature to let each municipality set its own speed limits—to drive motorists off the roads in sheer confusion. A Gorrie farmer demanded that cars be taxed up to $500 a year. The Ontario Liberal leader suggested in 1908 that autos be banned entirely from certain roads—which is precisely what happened in Prince Edward Island that year.

The Island, really just one oversize farm, had never liked cars from the day a second-hand Ford appeared in 1905. The 1908 act prohibited their use on any street, lane or highway at risk of a $500 fine or six months in jail. Even that, the Premier remarked in the legislature, was not going far enough!

Gradually the P.E.I. law relaxed to permit driving on Mondays, Wednesdays and Thursdays. Motorists sneaked into the boondocks to woo farmers with free rides or the tempting "Have your picture taken in a real automobile!" Yet in 1914 a Charlottetown doctor, upon missing his train, had to petition the Premier for permission to drive to Alberton to perform an emergency operation. He drove with a red cross fastened to his radiator, saved the patient's life, but was later threatened with prosecution. Only the transportation needs of wartime recruiters forced the Island to join the rest of North America and, by 1919, officially recognize the automobile.

This kind of boneheadedness brought about motor leagues in every province, as a matter of sheer survival. The members helped each other in roadside emergencies, erected road signs (which the farmers stubbornly pulled down or pointed the wrong way), lobbied for friendlier legislation and headed off such idiocy as a 1908 proposed amendment to the Criminal Code which would have made it an indictable offence, punishable by two years in prison, for a motorist to cause a horse to run away.

Drivers had enough grief without laws like that. The roads were almost impassable but this, in the beginning, was a lesser concern. Few cars had enough speed or range to get the owner very far; a drive around *town* was an achievement. Columnist J. V. McAree once recalled his first trip from Mimico to Oakville, Ont., about ten miles: "We kissed our wives tenderly. They bravely hid their tears. . . . We were venturing into the unknown . . . ."

Toronto's first Winton dealer, W. S. Smith, in 1902 thought nothing of spending three hours travelling the few blocks from home to office. He always carried a potato or two, for splicing broken fuel lines. Once he filled a flat tire with oats and water; the swollen grain kept the tire firm until he got home. Toronto's Dr. Perry Doolittle, an incredible quixotic character who became Canada's leading advocate of good roads (see Chapter 7), once filled *his* flat tire with milk and molasses. This worked for several weeks until one tire burst and the rancid mixture nearly asphyxiated him.

Doctor Perry E. Doolittle in his Stevens-Duryea, a gasoline-driven car.

A 1904 Rambler, from Hamilton.

There were perils from the moment a man turned the crank. Doolittle, who in 1899 bought Moodie's first Winton —which probably made him Canada's first used-car driver —had been told to start it with a quick turn. "Mr. Moodie did not say *two* quick turns," Doolittle related afterward, "so I gave it one and let it go at that, with the result that the flywheel carried it to compression and explosion, sending the piston backward and carrying the crank with it." It threw Doolittle on his back and sprained his wrist.

Breakdown and a tow home was so inevitable that one man built a whiffletree on his car front and carried harness with him. He was planning the ultimate in motoring security—a ring at the back so he could lead his *own* horse on every trip—when he died, unfulfilled.

Yet better times were on the way. City men were becoming charmed by the very aspect that farmers loathed —speed. The man who stirred their blood was Barney Oldfield—swashbuckling Barney of the lank black hair, bulldog jaw and total disregard for danger—whose name for twenty years would be synonymous with speed. He came to Toronto in September, 1904, for a series of racing exhibitions. Everybody knew how Oldfield, ex-bicycle rider, had learned to drive a car one week before he won his first race for Henry Ford. They ogled the "good looking young man with iron nerve and muscle." Every small boy knew about his apple-green Peerless racer, the Green Hornet, and how he crouched low over the wheel and *slid* through turns. And when he rocketed three miles in three minutes, $57\frac{2}{5}$ seconds, well, Toronto was at his feet. Speed!

The first auto race in Hamilton at the Jockey Club (1904).

More practical people were learning that cars were convenient and fairly inexpensive. A cheap runabout cost around $800, and doctors, in particular, found a smooth-starting car had it all over the horse for quick getaways on night calls. Gasoline was only seven to nine cents a gallon in some cities. A small gas buggy averaged $1\frac{3}{4}$ cents per mile in running costs. An electric cost one or two cents a mile; a steamer about $25 a month.

Finally, even if you weren't Barney Oldfield, there was exquisite pleasure just in driving. *The Canadian Magazine* summed it up as early as 1903: "The smooth skimming sensation, the delightful freshness of the never-failing breeze, the fascination of smoothly turned corners, and even the accompaniment played by the chug-chug of the gasoline car or the buzz of the electric, combine to make automobiling a recreation inferior to none and comparable to few. For it is recreation in the literal sense of the word. It really helps to create anew the businessman worn out with the nervous strain of office hours, or the busy doctor who could find time for no other amusement . . . ."

The Canadian and those persistent early motorists had discovered a basic fact of the twentieth century: the automobile for all its sins and frustrations was totally irresistible. Right then, although they wouldn't admit it for years, the farmers and other die-hards had lost, absolutely and forever. The horse was dead; long live the horseless.

An early automobile in the Canadian Rockies. Note the handles for the occupant of the "mother-in-law" seat to cling to.

2

"ALWAYS LET UP ON THE SPEEDER...."

Dr. Milton Good at 85 years of age. He was one of the original builders of the LeRoy.

The Stratford, Ont., shoe merchant Moses Schultzhauer must often have sprung from his bed in cold sweat that summer of 1901. He owned the world's first production model of a LeRoy automobile. For $650 he owned this amazing mechanical creature poised daintily outside his home: skinny wheels, mudguards arched like eyebrows, shin-high curving dashboard, kerosene lamps, everything. He was a lucky man—but what the devil did he do next?

Its manufacturers, Nelson Good and Dr. Milton Good of nearby Berlin (later Kitchener), had shown him how the LeRoy acted when aroused. It lurched ahead at speeds up to—Good God!—12 mph. It was therefore imperative that Moses Schultzhauer learn to drive. But how? Not one Canadian in a thousand had even *seen* an automobile.

Here, the genius of the brothers Good came to his aid; the instinctive self-cultivated genius that every pioneer car maker had. Their handy home-made LeRoy Instruction Book—24 pages of advice, diagrams and grim warnings (reproduced at the back of the book) spelled out everything Schultzhauer needed to know, *everything*, even how to drive. Nobody had told Milton, an M.D. with a passion for engines, or Nelson, an electrician and stationary engine expert, the best way to make or drive a car, because nobody knew for sure. With bits of technical lore gleaned from English and U.S. magazines, plus two years of harrowing experiments, they'd figured it out for themselves.

A blacksmith helped them build the car. Dunlop of Toronto made tires to their specifications. They invented terms: "speeder" (for accelerator), "back-up gear," "igniter plug." They devised an eleven-step lubrication procedure ("Fourth: Put three drops in each hole at the seven little hubs that project from the disk...."). They made up safety rules: "On approaching a team always let up on the

Lionel Rider in his LeRoy, which he completely restored. He discovered it in a bedroom above a bicycle shop, where it had been (in parts) for forty-four years.

speeder" and "Never make a quick turn of the steering lever while the vehicle is running at high speed; it is liable to cause a bad accident." They proudly named their car after the French *le roi* (king), a little touch of swank. Then they drove it to Michigan and back, getting it through customs by calling it farm machinery and taking the engine apart three times when it seized up.

After that, there wasn't much the Good brothers couldn't tell you about a LeRoy. And that was how cars were made at the turn of the century. The Goods and their contemporaries were the Columbuses and Magellans of auto making, prowling through vaguely charted worlds, inventing rules as they went along. And although fame eluded them and history ignored them, they made the way a little easier for those who followed.

Their booklet certainly made the way more interesting for student driver Schultzhauer. Motoring, he realized, was riddled with do's, don'ts and subtle hints of peril. He was cautioned to never "do anything to your motor without

STYLISH CAR COATS OF 1908:
Hooded Coat of Russian Pony

knowing just what you are doing." He was cheered to learn that, if the motor balked, "always consider that it *has* run, and will run again if conditions are the same. It is generally some trifling little thing that bothers." He was terrified by thinly-veiled threats: "Don't call in an automobile expert if you can avoid it. We know those experts"; "Never leave vehicle with motor running; a slight touch of the clutch lever will cause the carriage to leave you"; "Never fill gasoline reservoir by LAMPLIGHT." And he was relieved to find one easy rule: to check the gasoline level he simply stuck a pencil in the tank.

By page 24 Schultzhauer was ready for the list of skill-testing questions. "1. How do you start the motor?" Easy . . . well, it *looked* easy, on paper. You climbed up in the right-hand place, jiggled "the small rod just back of the seat," moved spark and switch levers forward, jammed a heel on the "relief lever" and reached down the right side to twirl the crank. If the relief lever was working, it prevented the LeRoy from backfiring and breaking your wrist. If *everything* was working, the mighty one-cylinder four-horsepower water-cooled engine came quiveringly alive beneath the seats.

And now: "2. How do you start the vehicle?" Good pupil Schultzhauer knew: by adjusting the spark, twiddling a fuel needle-valve, moving the clutch lever to SLOW (first of two forward speeds) and seizing the tiller, or "steering lever," with a death grip. As the booklet advised, Schultzhauer always kept "foot ready to apply the brake." Unfortunately, the brake was also the back-up pedal, which was the undoing of most LeRoy owners. To slow or stop, they literally threw the car into reverse, which often snapped the drive chain. More than one LeRoy driver discovered prayer while hurtling downhill with no controls except the tiller flapping in his hand.

Coat of Russian Pony and fur-lined sleeping bag.

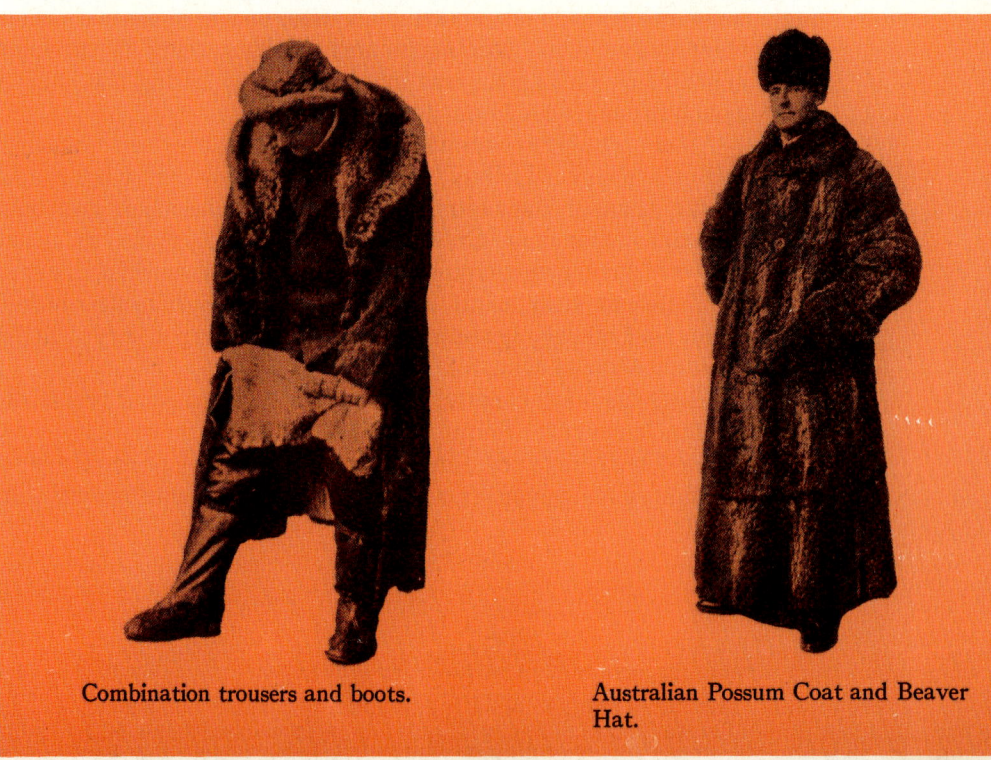

Combination trousers and boots.

Australian Possum Coat and Beaver Hat.

The caption for this photo appearing in the early 1900's was: "HANDSOME CAR BELONGING TO SENATOR COX. Nearly all of the most prominent men in Canada are becoming motor enthusiasts. This shows one of the fine cars that are used daily in Toronto."

Probably this is why Schultzhauer later sold LeRoy #1 and why a subsequent owner dismantled it in 1906, wrapped it in rags and stored it in an attic where it lay forgotten for forty-four years. Today it's in the Doon, Ont., pioneer museum. But the funny little LeRoy was a superior car for its time, so good that Ransom E. Olds, of the famous Oldsmobile and soon-to-be-famous Reo, came up from Michigan for an instructive day with its makers. The Goods turned out thirty-two LeRoys before they learned the harsh realities of Canadian auto making: the market was too small and U.S. competition too great for a native industry.

This didn't stop scores of other Canadians from trying. The Directory lists 93 models, but there may never be a truly accurate count of Canadian cars. For one thing, what *is* a "Canadian" car? Few were of *total* Canadian design or construction. Others, carbon copies of American models produced by Canadian affiliates, do not qualify. Probably the fairest criterion is any car that was produced here and was to some extent different, whether or not part of its financing or anatomy came from outside the country.

Automobile Ambulance

When your car gets hurt or takes sick on the road ---- **Phone North 1804**

I HAVE two 5-Ton Peerless Trucks always ready, day or night. Our Automatic Hoisting Bodies enable us to pick any kind of wreck.

COUNTRY TRIPS MY SPECIALTY

I also give the best prices on all kinds of Motor Truck Work. My Truck Bodies are suitable for any kind of material, and can dump a load in 60 seconds.

No one expects a breakdown, still they happen every day; so cut this out and carry it with you—it may prove a friend in need.

JAMES SERCOMBE

109 Lawton Ave.
TORONTO

Telephone North 1804

The Canadian Motorist, 1914.

Even this makeshift classification brings to light new candidates every time a book or article on the subject is published: obscure characters who built one or two models for their own amusement, people like Hambrecht of Kitchener and Mimna of Wardsville. In those first giddy years—from about 1900 to the late twenties—car making was a national game and anybody could play. Few of the players were manufacturers in the true sense, and most of them lost their shirts. A handful, such as Montreal's H. E. Bourassa, were talented inventors. Many were weekend tinkerers, eager to be first on their block with a motor car built from parts obtained by mail order. Still others were wheeler-dealers who built a prototype, gave it a name, incorporated, gathered up the shareholders' money and took the fastest conveyance—certainly not *their* car—out of town.

The rest were blacksmiths, farmers or carriage makers whose faith and sheer guts made up for their lack of mechanical talent. Faith was essential to anybody entering the business. As Ransom Olds later wrote of his own beginnings, "The prospects of the industry were not very bright .... The public persisted in the idea that it was not a practical proposition and would be a thing of the past within a year or two."

The Galt Storage-Gas-Electric ready for the road.

Their handiwork was as gloriously confused and individualistic as the makers themselves. When a neighbor said he had a new car, you hurried to look; it was quite possibly the first and last of its kind.

Cars clanked and wheezed out of barns, machine shops and buggy factories in nearly every province. The Davis was born in a Kingston shipyard; the Duplex came out of a Montreal ironworks. There were names like Crow, Iroquois, Ivanhoe, and Canadian Baby Car, a Montreal three-wheeler. From the carriage makers came styles called "landau," "cabriolet," "phaeton" and "brougham," as well as fringed tops, flower vases and robe rails.

There were gas buggies, steamers, electrics, plus the Galt gas-*and*-electric, with a gasoline engine that charged batteries which drove the car's electric motor; it could do 30 mph. The gasoline motors ranged from one to eight cylinders (including the Duplex with two pistons in each cylinder) and were variously driven by chain, shaft and friction. The lights, if any, were kerosene, water-and-carbide or, finally, electric. Bodies could be steel, wood, fabric-covered wood or, as in the London Six, aluminum over wood. The London Six was not popular with the aged, superstitious or frail of health: its frame was made by an Ingersoll casket maker.

There were one-seaters, two seaters and *dos-a-dos* (in which rear seat passengers faced backward). The 1901

View of the chassis and motor of the Galt Storage-Gas-Electric.

The Canadian Queen when owned by Gordon Edington of Toronto. Edington found it in parts in a garage in 1948 and completely reconstructed it. Here his parents are trying it out.

Mr. William Dobbie, the owner of the Glover, with his family. Dobbie obtained the parts from the U.S. and assembled the car with the help of Mr. Francis Wafer, a mechanic, who is here the proud driver of the car.

Queen runabout of Toronto had a fold-down spare seat ahead of the operator, thus creating the country's first official back seat driver.

At first, passengers boarded by steps at the side or back; later, by great wide running boards. They rolled on sometimes three but usually four steel tires or rubber tires (either solid or pneumatic) fixed to wheels with wooden or wire spokes. The Glover of Pincher Creek, Alta., had *five* wheels. Engines soon moved out from under the seats, beneath a lunch-box kind of hood with hinged sides. The earliest car tops were lofty open-sided canopies that flapped and billowed in the wind, threatening to whisk entire families away like Mary Poppins. There were electric horns that went EEENK and fat rubber bulbs hooked to trumpets that croaked AH-OOGHH. The Jules of Guelph would have delighted any modern cabbie: its horn button was in the middle of the brake pedal.

Antelope hunters, 1912, near Brooks, Alberta in a Franklin air-cooled C.P.R. car.

A Packard touring car in 1912 on the Peigan Indian Reserve. Chief Butcher is in the front passenger's seat.

Until World War I any Canadian or U.S. car might have bar, tiller or wheel steering, but nearly always on the right. This legacy from England made sense in British Columbia and the Maritimes where driving on the left was law. Elsewhere it only added to a motorist's misery. He could never see around a vehicle to pass, and his passengers had to load and unload in the dirty street instead of the sidewalk.

Manufacturers argued that a driver *had* to sit on the right; how else could he keep an eye on the ditch? Also, if he sat on the left, where would they put gear shift, brake lever and horn assembly which, with right-hand drive, were all positioned *outside* along with the spare tire and tool box? Actually, when left-hand drive became universal, the motorist managed nicely with controls inside and spare parts stowed elsewhere. Until then, the right front door was so useless that in many cars it was actually a dummy.

Freakish, ludicrous, laughable now, those early autos nevertheless had "modern" features that we arrogantly assume could only be products of our generation. As early as 1908 Dunlop made three kinds of non-skid tire tread: wire mesh, cross-grooved and rubber-studded. A Niagara Falls firm sold a winter outer tread studded with rivets and snapped over the conventional tire with coil-spring fasteners.

The Bartlett used pneumatic rubber cushions instead of steel spring. Chatham's Gray-Dort had an automatic back-up light in the twenties, and in 1906 the Russell of Toronto had its gear shift—three speeds forward and one reverse—mounted on the steering column.

The Russell, in fact, was thoroughly admirable, one of the few to make a serious bid for survival in the early years. It was a product of the Canada Cycle and Motor Company, already famous for bicycles and for the 1903 Ivanhoe electric.

Russell cars on display in front of Toronto City Hall.

The road to Banff from Calgary in 1913.

It was named after Tommy Russell, CCM's vice-president and general manager, who probably owed his success to the fact that he was *not* a mechanic or village blacksmith. Russell was a recent honors graduate in political science from the University of Toronto, young, blunt, aggressive, slow to smile, impatient with small talk. A contemporary writer noted proudly, "He does not mope, neither does he write poetry." (In other words: Take heart, Mr. 1905 Businessman; Russell is no limp-wristed intellectual!) But although Russell was "clear in the eye and strong in the limb, with a shoving football gait," he evidently used his brains more than his biceps.

A Russell with a Knight sleeve-valve engine, about 1912, and right, the luxurious five-passenger electric brougham presented to Mrs. Borden, the wife of the Right Hon. R. L. Borden, Prime Minister of Canada.

A GREAT WAY TO GO

Taylor Steam Buggy, 1867. Built by Henry Seth Taylor of Stanstead, Quebec.

1908 McLaughlin.

1907 Tudhope-McIntyre.

1909 Tudhope.

1909 Ford tourer. Owned by Ronald Fawcett, Whitby.

Very rare coloured cover picture of a 1910 Ford of Canada catalogue.

One of the few 1916 Bartletts in existence today is in the Antique Auto Museum, Niagara Falls, Ontario.

Late model McKay—about 1914.

The Russell was an idea car. As well as gear shift on the steering column, it had two kerosene lights *plus* a water-carbide driving light, adjustable to any angle. The handbrake, when pulled on, automatically disengaged the transmission even when the car was in gear.

Later, with exclusive Canadian rights to the Knight sleeve-valve engine from America, CCM produced four-and six-cylinder models at $1,475 to $3,000. It was high for the times but Russell stressed quality ("Made Up to a Standard —Not Down to a Price") and sales were still healthy when World War I broke out. Then the firm went into munitions and Russell-Knight never came back from war.

Meanwhile the Comet, Montreal's first production model, had a gallant two-year fling, backed by Quebec money. If nothing else it was surely the most cosmopolitan machine in Canada: Italian engine, a French rear axle, a German front axle, American radiator and a canvas-covered wooden body made in Quebec. The highlight of its little life was in hauling the Prince of Wales during his visit to the province. A car fit for His Royal Highness might have caught on in blue-blood Toronto or Loyalist Kingston, but it didn't impress Quebec.

In 1908, while the Comet was fizzling out, the brothers Jack and Dan McKay, transplanted Prince Edward Islanders then living in Kentville, N.S., took a whirl at the auto game. With no knowledge whatsoever, they rented a carriage company, surveyed the field and decided to create their own version of the Penn, a Pittsburgh model.

Early model McKay—about 1911.

"Everitt" cars 1911: (left) Five-passenger standard touring model; (right) Three-passenger inside control coupe model. Made by Tudhope.

They bought enough U.S. parts for twenty-five cars, set their carriage makers to building wooden bodies and brought in brother Stan from the Island. Stan lent a certain technical authority to the enterprise: he was a blacksmith. In two years the McKays produced many sleighs and carriages and twenty-five McKay cars. Then Amherst, 220 miles away, lured the firm to "Nova Scotia's new industrial capital."

After a shaky start (their new four-storey building threatened to collapse even before it was finished) the brothers were back in business with dreams as bright as the McKay's nickel trim. Surprisingly, it was a fine car, and soon earned local fame by winning a 425-mile road race, Halifax to Yarmouth and return. The four-cylinder 30-horsepower model had a mahogany dash, a steering wheel, leather upholstery, silk mohair top, windshield, speedometer, gas headlights, side oil lamps, shock absorbers, good brakes and an electric self-starter—all for $2,050.

It would have been a bargain in most places but even the $1,450 roadster was too high priced for the average Nova Scotian in 1913-1914. Short of operating capital, plagued by the public's increasing insistence on ever-changing styles, the McKays finally went under when World War I pinched off their supplies. They shut down after producing 100 cars in two years, instead of the hoped-for 1,000 a year.

Theirs was only one of many car companies killed by the war, but they went out with characteristic flair. When Prince Edward Island's ban on motoring eased off, during mobilization, the McKays saw a magnificent sales chance in their homeland. One of them jumped in a car and sped toward the Island for the honor and publicity of being "first on the Island" after the auto famine. A Buick got there first—the kind of rotten luck that dogged the brothers to the end.

A little luck—good or bad—made all the difference. The Tudhopes of Orillia had some of each. As respected long-time carriage makers, with a plant covering three blocks and an annual payroll of $100,000, they had a sounder base for car manufacture than most competitors. They also shrewdly

When the value of motor vehicles was realized, trucks of every size and shape appeared.

guessed that skeptical Canadians still needed a gentle transition from horse to horseless. Their 1906 two-cylinder Tudhope-McIntyre, with an air-cooled engine from Indiana, looked comfortably like a high-wheeled carriage.

By 1909 the $550 Tudhope gave thirty miles to the gallon with a top speed of 25 mph, had solid rubber tires and could go "over any kind of road, up any hill, that any horse can pull a buggy." But it still had a buggy top, black body with red trim, and was called a "motor carriage."

Then one August Saturday afternoon, fire raged through the plant and much of the downtown business section. The little fire departments of Orillia and nearby Barrie couldn't cope. Only the company records (locked in a safe), a few auto frames and 150 sets of carriage wheels were saved.

Was it the end of Tudhope—indeed, of Orillia? The town revolved around the company. Nineteen other communities eagerly tried to coax the Tudhopes away. Orillia offered a $50,000 no-interest twenty-year loan. "Our company doesn't want charity or handouts," owner J. B. Tudhope assured the cheering town council, on accepting its offer. "I look upon the arrangement as a straight business proposition. We will give good value for what we receive."

They did. A week after the fire, a bigger and better plant was going up. By winter it was in business. With it came the first distinct automobile division, Tudhope Motor Company, which initially sold the four-cylinder $1,250 Everitt from the U.S. Tudhope was a craftsman and perfectionist. He didn't just assemble U.S. parts: he made the entire chassis, motor and transmission with his own machines, dies and 782 jigs, to tolerances of 1/1000 of an inch. When Everitt went out of business in 1911, Tudhope made his own automobile: "The Car Ahead—Just One Step Ahead of the Horse." (Even then he refused to ridicule the horse and buggy set; he was still building carriages for them, too.)

Packard Electric factory in St. Catharines assembled various American cars during different periods. Here are completed and partially completed Oldsmobiles in front of the factory.

The Tudhope was several steps ahead of most other cars. In 1913 it offered shock absorbers, a gasoline gauge (many autos still relied on a dipstick), a genuine mohair top, a brass-trimmed plate glass windshield, electric starter and electric lights—all as standard equipment. The body, dark blue with French gray, had seats of hand-buffed leather, wide enough in the back for "three large passengers." But at prices up to $2,500 sales tapered off. With the war, Tudhope turned to making military supplies and never went back to "The Car Ahead."

So they were all gone now—Tudhope, Comet, Russell, McKay. Gone, too, were the short-lived Chatham, Menard, Acme, Kennedy and many, many more. Only one of the major all-Canadian pioneers was financially alive and well, the only man in the country to fully understand and cope with the bitter economic facts of Canadian automaking, the ex-carriage-maker with "wheels in his head": Mr. Sam McLaughlin. His story was an object lesson to all the rest.

A rare photo showing the interior of the Oldsmobile factory.

3

WHEELS IN HIS HEAD

As the verse on McLaughlin's 1908 calendar told it: "The sun was shining brightly on a summer day in June, When this happy wedded couple started on their honeymoon. And a very cogent reason for their happiness is seen, For they both begin their journey in a Model Seventeen. It is thus in every journey—nothing ill can e'er befall, While McLaughlin-Buick motor cars bring happiness to all."

And there was the bride with her little rosebud mouth; the groom in his boiled white shirt; the well-wishers in top hats and long gowns, posed stiff as Dresden figurines; the church, parson and lacy French-impressionist trees—the whole idyllic Good-Old-Days wedding. Except . . . there, to whisk them away on this tender June morning, was a great rangy brass-trimmed cherry-red touring car!

Surely this little touch must have baffled the recipients of McLaughlin Carriage Company's annual calendar. In the previous two years the calendar had starred smug couples in McLaughlin horse-drawn carriages, highstepping it past

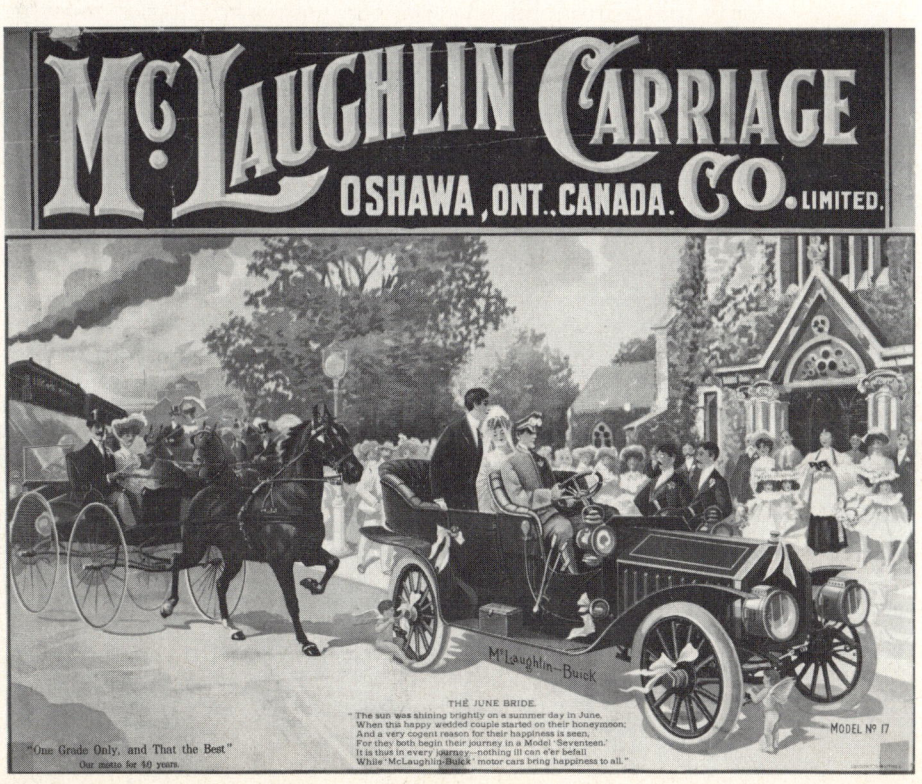

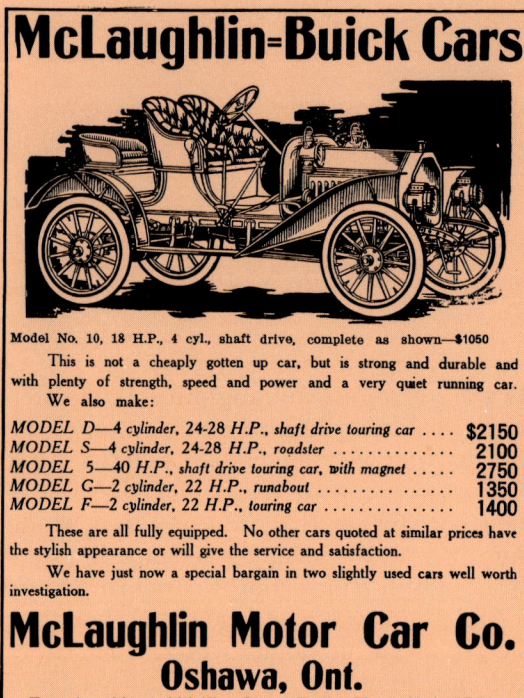

fools whose evil erratic motor cars had dumped them in ditches or dunked them in streams. Had the McLaughlins of Oshawa, backbone of Canada's carriage trade, done a complete about-face? They had. And right there is the turning point in the story of Robert Samuel McLaughlin, Canada's only real automobile tycoon, the man who did the most to create General Motors of Canada.

His is a classic tale of a village boy who apprenticed in his father's carriage shop, worked hard, believed in such old-fashioned virtues as quality and a square deal, built a corporation, became a millionaire-philanthropist, and lived happily a long time after. It is about a man who, like many, anticipated the triumph of the motor car but, like no other Canadian, knew when to fight the Yankees and when to join them.

Sixty-one years after that turnabout-by-calendar, Mr. Sam sits in his big corner office at General Motors, Oshawa, on the verge of his ninety-eighth birthday but still GM's chairman of the board and still as tough and durable as the imported mahogany he put into those first cars.

He is a blunt but endearing old gentleman in a tan suit and brown tie, wearing GM's 50-years'-service diamond cufflinks (which is a bit ludicrous since he has been in service eighty-two years), the raspy voice still strong, the eyes still alert behind spectacles. He thwacks his torso with a fist, unflinchingly, and says proudly, "Look at that! I exercise, hard, every morning. Come here. Feel that arm." His biceps are hard. He comes to the office every morning when he's in Oshawa "to keep an eye on things." But mostly, now, it is memories, and he likes to talk about those momentous early years. "It's been a very interesting life," he says. And *that* is the understatement of the century.

Robert McLaughlin.

Robert Samuel McLaughlin was born in 1871 in Enniskillen, a village near Oshawa, third son of an Irish carriage maker. At age five the boy wandered into the shop where freshly painted carriage wheels hung drying from the ceiling. One fell on his head and knocked him flat. His father silenced his howling by popping a brown striped "humbug" candy into his mouth and from then on the family joked that Sam had "wheels in his head." And, in fact, he thought about carriage wheels, bicycle wheels, car wheels for the rest of his life. This affection for carriages was a direct legacy from his father, "The Governor," as the boys called him. The Governor loved the smell and feel of wood being shaped under his chisels. Proud, scrupulously fair, he settled only for the finest upholstery, the truest grain of wood and imported Norway iron that cost five or ten times more than any other.

People respected his quality. The carriage business outgrew its facilities. McLaughlin moved to Oshawa, built a three-storey shop and forge, pursued his quest for better

Robert McLaughlin (third from left) with his workmen in front of his Oshawa Carriage Works, built in 1867.

Early McLaughlin calendar pictures which show the change in emphasis from carriages to automobiles.

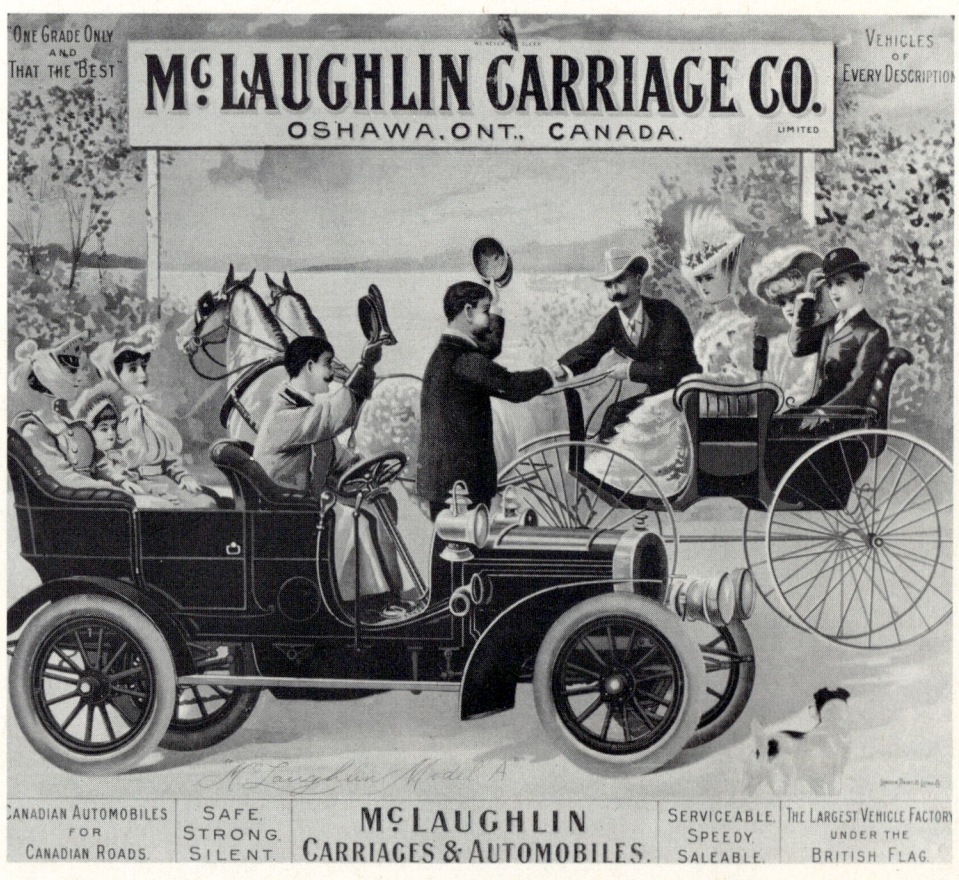

carriages and suddenly found himself mildly famous. He invented a new "gear," carriage terminology for everything between body and wheels (springs, chassis, couplings and the mechanism that permitted the front axle to turn and so steer the vehicle). McLaughlin's gear featured a fifth wheel that made carriages safer and smoother riding.

One day he brought home momentous news.

"Boys," he announced, "I have had an offer to sell the gear patent. Ten thousand dollars! Will I take it?"

> Mr. Sam leans back in a cloud of pipe smoke (Barking Dog pipe mixture, two tins standing ready on a table behind him). "Ten thousand dollars was a lot of money, then. But with one accord we said 'No'. I was just a kid. But we were all so proud of him for getting that patent. We just didn't want him to part with it."

So the Governor kept it but he sold exclusive distributing rights. Carriage factories all over the country advertised their products as "equipped with the wonderful new McLaughlin gear." This in turn brought a nation-wide demand for the entire McLaughlin carriage. Once more the Governor's shop was crowded.

Despite this environment of success and respect, Sam, on finishing high school at sixteen, didn't intend to go into the carriage business. His oldest brother Jack, a graduate chemist from the University of Toronto, was already in New York, on the way to *his* life's achievement: founding the Canada Dry beverage company. Brother George was apprenticed to the carriage shop, and one more carriage maker in the family seemed enough. Sam thought of being a hardware merchant, lawyer, draftsman, maybe even a champion bicycle rider. He rode his highwheeler everywhere—a sixteen-mile workout every day; sometimes to Toronto and back, sixty miles in a day; and once to Brockville, a 300-mile round trip. He entered races at fall fairs and was forever winning cups, plaques and pickle dishes.

But brother Jack spoke sternly about family responsibilities and in 1887 Sam became an apprentice upholsterer. As the owner's son he had the privilege of sweeping floors. The staff worked a fifty-nine hour week; Sam worked six days a week from seven until seven. (He was thirty and a partner in the business before he finally had the nerve to go to work at 8:00 A.M. and then was so guilt-ridden that he sneaked in the back door.)

Apprentice McLaughlin earned $3.00 a week, of which the Governor deducted $2.50 for room and board. He learned to stitch and make cushions, graduated to journeyman at $1.75 a day, and quit. Sam had to be sure he wasn't riding on the Governor's coattails. At Watertown, N.Y.,

The disastrous fire of 1899, which completely destroyed the McLaughlin Carriage Company.

he landed a job with a carriage company and drew top wages. He moved on through Syracuse and Binghampton, holding his own everywhere and soaking up knowledge from the best carriage makers in the east. Then he blew all his savings in New York City and went home to become foreman of the family shop.

"I also found out our designs were way behind the U.S. I'd taken a correspondence course in drafting so now I designed a new carriage. Father said, 'Sam you go ahead and do all the designing'. And from then on I did."

The McLaughlins now offered 143 carriage and sleigh designs, with many new models every year. Quebec liked the Concord bodies; Ontario favored boxlike shapes; the west called for buckboards and democrats; city people and Maritimers demanded handsome phaetons, Stanhopes and fringe-top surreys.

Often Sam worked until after midnight, reshaping a design on paper until he liked it. Then he transferred the drawings to blackboards and the foremen relayed them into prototypes. It was training that would soon serve him well in auto making.

An accident moved him one step nearer the car business. In December, 1899, the plant burned to the ground. Like most buildings then, it was a fire hazard and like most fire departments Oshawa's couldn't handle much more than a chimney blaze. It wiped out the raw materials; the finished

After the fire temporary quarters were set up at Gananoque, shown here.

and half-finished carriages; the tools and jigs; all of Sam's designs, and jobs for 600 men.

The McLaughlin name was still intact: sixteen towns clamoured to have the carriage company come to them. The McLaughlins liked Oshawa, though, and the love affair was mutual. With a $50,000 loan from the town, to be repaid "as convenient," the family rebuilt, while holding their customers with temporary production from a makeshift plant 150 miles away.

The new factory was as exciting as the new century: two big buildings covering more than 40,000 square feet; five-inch floors; an underground water tank with pump; a generator for electric light, and telephones to replace the old signal system of whistling and hollering down a metal pipe. They hired a stenographer. Sam and George now had executive assistants. Oliver Hezzlewood, the local school teacher, became consulting bookkeeper and accountant. The company volume reached 25,000 carriages that year and sales passed $1 million. This was progress. And suddenly more progress came sputtering along the roads, scaring the devil out of McLaughlin carriage drivers' horses.

> "First car I ever rode in was a wee little thing, Hezzlewood's. It might have been a Ford. I designed a kind of rain cape for it—there was no top—so the passengers could sit under it with their heads poked through. Right then I knew cars were bound to come. I knew we had to get a car company."

The C. C. Short family of High River, Alberta, with their McLaughlin touring car in 1910.

But the Governor loathed the new contraptions and Sam had to disguise his hunch. He went on "summer vacation" to Buffalo, and called on Richard Pierce, whose Pierce-Arrow was already synonymous with speed and elegance. Pierce took him to lunch and around his plant, then said quietly, "This kind of car has no future, Mr. McLaughlin. I would advise you against trying to make them." He was right; the Pierce-Arrow, priced as high as $7,300, was never a mass-appeal car, although it survived until 1938. Sam got the message: his family could make low-priced quality carriages for the mass market; they should try the same with cars, if try they must.

He went on to Buffalo's Thomas Flyer plant, Peerless in Cleveland, Reo in Lansing. Later that year, he and Hezzlewood, now a full-time company employee, called on the Jackson auto plant in Michigan. There, in a hotel dining room, they ran into William Crapo Durant, new boss of Buick and a legendary figure in the story of North American motoring.

> "He was a great, great friend of mine. We first met at a carriage makers' convention in Philadelphia in 1896; I already knew his son-in-law. After that I saw him often, right up until his death in 1947. I never took the liberty of calling him anything but 'Mr. Durant,' I respected him so much."

"Sam! What are you doing here?" Durant said, that day in 1906. Looking for a deal to make Jackson cars in Canada, McLaughlin explained. Durant looked dubious. "If you're not satisfied with what you see, come to me," he urged.

McLaughlin made tentative arrangements to make the Jackson, subject to a test drive. He ordered a chain-driven and shaft-driven model shipped to Oshawa. When they arrived he and Hezzlewood went out on the roads. In an hour both cars broke down several times. There was just one more possibility: Durant.

W. C. Durant was already variously hated, loved or grudgingly admired by everybody in the fledgling United States auto business. He had no technical knowledge or mechanical skill, but the nerve of a burglar and an insatiable appetite for work. To some he was an arrogant tyrant who loved to make his retainers jump. To others he was simply a brilliant entrepreneur who, unluckily, couldn't administrate. But everybody agreed that Durant truly loved the great new automobile game and played it harder and better than most. Writers reported, only partly in jest, that Durant believed the smallest form of currency was the one thousand dollar bill. McLaughlin says Durant made and lost at least two fortunes.

A 1912 McLaughlin.

Durant was to die bankrupt but when Mr. Sam approached him he was a millionaire carriage maker who had won control of Buick and was about to make a greater impact on the American industry than anyone with the possible exception of Ford. Over twenty years, Durant put Buick into the black, started Chevrolet, helped keep Oldsmobile, Oakland (later Pontiac) and Cadillac alive. He brought Walter Chrysler into Buick and *he* went on to create Plymouth and Chrysler. This was Sam McLaughlin's friend and soon-to-be business associate.

Before McLaughlin contacted Durant, though, he swore he wouldn't repeat the Jackson fiasco. He bought a $1,650 two-cylinder Model F Buick in Toronto, started back toward Oshawa for the road test and immediately knew it was the car he wanted. He called on Durant, spent two and a half days studying Buick's plant, then sat down to work out financial details. It was a dead end. They couldn't agree on the final terms and at last parted, still friends but unbending.

"Sorry we couldn't work it out," McLaughlin said.

"So am I," said Durant. "This is the car for you."

Stubbornly McLaughlin went back to make an all-Canadian car. His brother was enthusiastic. The Governor said simply, "If you boys think you can do it, go ahead." They found a first class engineer in Arthur Milbrath of a Milwaukee engine firm. They fitted a shop with automatic lathes, planers, shapers, dozens of machines.

> "When we started, we *really* made cars. We had crankshafts and cylinders and pistons forged in Cleveland to our specifications. I got busy on the design. Our carriage designs had been superior to anything else—good honest fine carriages with styles. And that's how we were going to build cars."

Everything was ready for the first one hundred, down to a handsome brass radiator bearing the McLaughlin name, when Arthur Milbrath fell ill with pneumonia. The McLaughlins were helpless without him. Sam wired Durant: could he lend them an engineer? Back came Durant's reply. "I'm coming over tomorrow."

Durant arrived early in the morning, a small spare man with dark brown piercing eyes. He brought no engineer—but two of his top executives. Again he wanted to make a deal.

> "He showed me that it was futile to make cars a hundred at a time. He showed me this is a volume business and if you didn't have volume you were dead. Him telling me that was the turning point in our history."

Durant also had a better offer, closer to McLaughlin's original proposal. In five minutes they drew up a one and one-half page contract, giving the McLaughlins 15-year rights to the Buick engine. They would design and build the bodies. Any regret McLaughlin had about not producing a completely Canadian car was outweighed by reality. All around him, auto makers were failing and, once having failed, rarely came back. The McLaughlins had teamed up with a good engine maker and their cars, like their carriages, were "One Grade Only and That The Best."

> "I really made that first car a hot one! I imported black material from England for the top, East African mahogany for the instrument panels, fine wood for the bodies. We brought in beautiful wool upholstery from England and leather and cords. Always the best."

1908 McLaughlin Model F.

One of the early McLaughlin-Buicks is now on display in Oshawa's automotive museum: a proud red beast with wooden steering wheel on the right side, padded bucket seats in front, a side crank, noble headlights and a windshield standing tall as a six-footer's head.

The McLaughlins turned out nearly 200 that first year, 423 by 1909, 1098 by 1914. For a while, on their advertising man's advice, they changed the name to Buick, to capitalize on its United States popularity. Sales immediately dropped. "McLaughlin" still meant quality to Canadians, and the cars became McLaughlin-Buicks again.

As such they bore the designer's distinctive touch. Once at GM's request, a McLaughlin-Buick went on display in New York. Admiring crowds gathered in the showroom. "Get that thing out of here!" snapped a GM vice president. "It's no more like our Buicks than a St. Bernard is like a dachshund!"

Sam McLaughlin was now president of the McLaughlin company and a director of General Motors. GM was a Durant original: not long after his deal with the McLaughlins he put together Buick, Oakland, Oldsmobile, Cadillac, the Champion spark plug company and assorted other truck companies and makers of minor automobiles or accessories—twenty-five in all.

> Sam knew them all—the great, near-great or soon-to-be-great. "Ransom Olds, DuPont, Sloan ... Louis Chevrolet, nice chap, big heavy fellow, always good natured ... Walter Chrysler, I knew him intimately, we used to go to the lake together with our wives; he was a fine manufacturer ... Tommy Russell, he was a smart businessman ... But Mr. Durant made the most impression on me. None of the others, in my estimation, reached his stature."

Col. R. S. McLaughlin at his desk.

Walter Chrysler.

Louis Chevrolet.

Henry Ford.

William C. Durant.

One of the first McLaughlin cars.

As a GM director and Durant's friend, Mr. Sam also had a hand in historic decisions, including—in a roundabout way—setting up a future competitor. One day, casually discussing with Durant a replacement for a Buick general manager who was ill, Sam said, "How about Charlie Nash?" Nash, then general manager of the Durant Dort Carriage Company, got the job, became president of General Motors, later went on to form the Nash Motor Company, which was in turn the foundation of American Motors.

On another memorable day in 1909 McLaughlin almost helped rewrite automobile history. Durant called his directors together to vote on a proposal: he had a forty-eight-hour option to buy the entire Ford Motor Company for $9.2 million. A banking group had tentatively agreed to back him. Fine, agreed McLaughlin and the other directors. But the backers backed out. The auto industry was fluttering like a barometer; Henry Ford hadn't made his name, and his company, the bankers ruled, wasn't worth the price.

Durant himself was soon under so much financial strain that bankers had to lend $15 million to bail GM out. Durant, under the terms, had to relinquish his management. That, of course, was no way to keep him out of the auto game. He bobbed up again with the French racing drivers, Louis and Arthur Chevrolet, made Arthur his chauffeur and set Louis to the drawing board. Soon Louis' car, with Durant heading the company, was on its way to the top.

Discussing the new Chevrolets with Durant over lunch in New York one day, McLaughlin said, "I hear you're going to produce some of them in West Toronto. How's the project going? It'll be tough competition for us."

Before Durant could answer, one of their companions, a Chevrolet stockholder, said, "Why don't you give Canadian Chevy to the McLaughlin boys, Billy?"

Durant, who was soon to resume leadership of GM, grinned. "Do you want it, Sam?"

McLaughlin did. But would it jeopardize his contract with Buick? And would the Governor agree to sell the carriage business? (The McLaughlins couldn't take on a new car and keep carriages.) Durant gave him two days to find out.

Brother George came down to help study the details. A GM legal expert assured them their Buick contract would not suffer. But what about the Governor? The brothers returned to Oshawa. "I can't face him," George said. So Sam McLaughlin braced himself for the most painful confrontation of his life.

"McLaughlin" in script appeared on the early cars.

> "I explained that the carriage business would be dead in three or four years, we had the figures to prove it. I said we had to go wholly into motor cars if we were going to stay in business. He took it quietly. He said, 'I'm about through. If you boys think it's wise, then all right.' I went out and called my friend Tudhope of Orillia and sold the carriage business that very day. We met the next morning in Toronto in the Queen's Hotel to close the deal. They bought us out holus-bolus. It was all gone in two months."

With 1918 came the last painful decision: the outright sale to General Motors. Sam McLaughlin had no sons. Neither George nor his sons wanted to continue. The Governor (who died in 1921) was less and less interested in the business.

> "He was quite a good oil painter, he could have been a great one. He used to bring his easel to the office every day and work. He liked to go into the woodworking shop, too; he still loved the smell and feel of wood. . . ."

The McLaughlin name plate prior to 1924. The porcelain name plate evolved from the name in script across the radiator. After 1924 "Buick" was added to the lower half of the diamond.

In 1929 company executives pose with Mr. McLaughlin in the 1908 Model F.

1925 McLaughlin-Buick.

The Buick contract would soon expire and could never be renewed on such favorable terms. GM would surely not let the McLaughlins keep Chevrolet alone. For McLaughlin to go on his own in Canada would be commercial suicide. On the other hand, if he accepted the GM offer Oshawa would always have a motor industry—and Oshawa deserved it.

So McLaughlin sold but stayed as president of General Motors of Canada and, until 1967, a director of General Motors Corporation.

A famous Canadian Buick: The City of Ottawa presented this car to Barbara Ann Scott (now Mrs. Thomas V. King) in 1947.

His worth has been estimated at $100 million. In latter years he has given at least $10 million in gifts to hospitals, universities and other charities. A planetarium in Toronto bears his name. He lives with his household staff in a twelve-acre estate with eleven greenhouses and superb gardens. He goes south in the winter; likes to play dominoes and watch TV; has several cars ("The Buick's my running-around car. They'd shoot me if I didn't have a Buick!"). But his wife and all those friends of the great days are gone and it is a little lonely.

Less than most of us, but with more right than any of us, he likes to reminisce. His chauffeur is waiting ("Haven't touched a steering wheel myself in forty-four years. Too much trouble parking in places like Toronto.") but he buzzes for his pretty secretary to bring in catalogues of cars and carriages from long ago. An aide springs to attention and cries, "I'll get them," but McLaughlin, with a grin and a glint in his eye, says, "No, she'll bring 'em. I like to look at *her*, too."

Then he says, "Come around here," and lovingly traces the dainty designs with a finger: "Look at that! And that one! They were beautiful." And they were. He leans back, pipe fuming, and looks around at the memorabilia of his life: plaques, scrolls of honor, a framed photo of The Governor, one of The Governor's oil paintings, framed prints of the calendars that marked the McLaughlin transition from carriages to cars. "One Grade Only and That The Best," he repeats softly. "That was our secret."

There was only one grade of Sam McLaughlin, too—the best.

Col. McLaughlin with Queen Mother Elizabeth in 1965 at E. P. Taylor's farm.

4

AND THE LITTLE FORD RAMBLED RIGHT ALONG

The Model T Ford was never *just* an automobile. It was a legend almost from the moment it was built; an international joke; a thing alternately beloved and hated by anyone who owned it. It was the epitome of standardization and mass production. Yet the owners swore that no T was quite like any other, that *their* T quivered, snuffled, nudged and forever threatened to prance away on its own, like a living creature. No other car in history so stirred the emotions or so effectively sealed the human love affair with the "horseless." For an entire generation of Canadians, as well as Americans, the T was a way of life.

A 1926 Model T Ford, four-cylinder, two-passenger coupe.

It was variously known as the Tin Lizzie, Detroit Disaster and Mechanical Cockroach. Whole joke books were written about it ("I hear Henry's painting all his Model T's yellow." "How come?" "He's gonna sell 'em in bunches like bananas."). It added the word "flivver" to our language, derived from the joke that a rattling ride in a T was good "for the liver," and defined in one dictionary as "a small and inexpensive automobile; hence anything that is small of its kind and cheap or insignificant." Small and cheap it was; insignificant the Model T was not. Its owners submitted it to awful indignities; loaded and drove it beyond all reason; yet for eighteen years, while other cars came and went, the little old Ford (as one of the scores of Model T songs put it) just rambled right along.

It was by no means the exclusive property of America. From the beginning, the Model T was made in Windsor and sometimes minor innovations appeared here before the United States market. Between 1908 and 1927, 750,000 Canadians bought new Tin Lizzies and thousands more bought second hand.

By 1914, for instance, 38 per cent of the cars sold in this country were Fords. Who bought them? Let us stroll through the purple prose of the 1914 Ford *Times*. Here is William "Dad" Yates of Hope, B.C., for one, nearly 100 years old but having his first car ride. His wizened whiskery little face peers out from—yes! a Ford!— and says (perhaps with a little push from the district salesman), "It's more comfortable to ride in a Model T than on the hurricane deck of a cayuse!" Here, sturdy and tall among his pure-bred Holsteins, stands F. R. Mallory of Port Hope, Ont., avowing, "There are only two cars for the farmer:

A typical billboard ad showing a 1927 Ford sport roadster.

the Ford and the Can't Afford." And here—oh, what hath Ford wrought?—are the Royal Canadian Mounted Police of Regina ("these picked men, clean of limb, fearless in heart and hard as nails from their life in the open") turning in their faithful steeds for $30,000 worth of Fords: "On those wonderful Prairie trails an officer can shoot out and lug back some boisterous disturber—sixty miles there and back—in a couple of hours. With the more picturesque horse it means a day and a night ride."

From coast to coast the testimonials rolled in. In those days Canadians felt Ford was as much their own as, say, Russell or McLaughlin-Buick. Hadn't Ford of Canada been in business ten years, only a year less than Henry's original company? And, in fact, hadn't the initiative for Ford of Canada come from *this* side of the border?

In 1904 Gordon McGregor, manager of his family's Walkerville Wagon Works (in what is now east Windsor) anticipated the ultimate triumph of the automobile.

"People like Ford say every farmer will soon have one," McGregor mused. "Why can't we build them here? I'm going to see John Curry." Curry, a local banker, was interested enough to cross the river with McGregor and see Ford.

Henry Ford was well on his way to becoming a resident American folk-hero. The one-time farm boy—who quit school at sixteen and still couldn't spell precisely or read freely—was brimming with energy, mechanical talent and visions of a car for the common people. His lieutenant was Canadian-born James Couzens, a managerial wizard so cool and tough that even the cantankerous Ford couldn't stare him down. It was said that when Couzens released his annual smile the ice in Lake Erie cracked from shore to shore.

They were a good match: the cranky single-minded visionary and the hardheaded organization man. Couzens guided Ford through the rocks and shoals of industry and finance where lesser auto makers foundered. And though

A Model T near Englehart, Ontario, about 1915; (right) a "turtle-deck" Model T finds it slow going.

The Walkerville Wagon Works, Walkerville, Ontario, the original plant of the Ford Motor Company of Canada, Limited.

Ford was only a year into his own business McGregor sensed a winner. He got the Canadian and British Commonwealth Ford franchise and secured backing in Canada. On August 17, 1904, Ford of Canada was founded with McGregor as general manager, a job he held until his death in 1922.

Even McGregor couldn't have dreamed that he was spawning one of Canada's "Big Three": an automaker that sixty-six years later would have subsidiaries in Australia, New Zealand, South Africa and Malaysia, an annual payroll of nearly $150 million, plants in four Ontario cities and a lifetime output of about six million vehicles.

The Walkerville Wagon Works "assembly plant" was a mess, its floor four inches thick with paint drippings, its walls a crazy quilt of color from paint brush wipings. The only power machinery was a drill press, subsequently driven by the rear wheel of a Ford. The office staff was one stenographer and one bookkeeper. But in October, while the seventeen employees cheered, McGregor drove the first Model C down Sandwich Street.

Canadian production crept along: 110 cars in the first year, only 486 by 1908. Then Ford brought out the Model T. According to the Ford legend, now almost as revered in America as the life stories of Lincoln or Daniel Boone, Henry had always dreamed of an Everyman's car. A Ford of Canada 1914 booklet quoted that dream, in language suspiciously like a copywriter's: "I will build a motor car for the multitude. It shall be large enough for the family but small enough for the unskilled individual to easily operate— and it shall be light in weight that it may be economical in maintenance. It will be built of honest materials—by the best workmen that money can hire—after the simplest designs that modern engineering can devise. But it shall be so low in price that the man of moderate means may own one—and enjoy with his family the blessings of happy hours spent in God's great open spaces."

The Model T was all of these things. It weighed 1200 pounds, had a four cylinder, 20-horsepower motor and could reach 40 mph. From a distance it resembled a black top hat on wheels. Fuel feed was by gravity from a tank under the seat; when gas was low, the driver had to *back* up steep hills to keep it flowing; when the tank was dry he had to uproot the seat for a refill. There was no water pump; Ford clung to the principle that warm water rises by itself. The first basic model had a chassis, four wheels, four tires, oil lamps for the sides and rear—and no more. Spare tire, windshield, top gas head and lights were extras. For years, so were speedometer, starter, temperature gauge and bumpers. Soon a whole sub-industry of Model T accessories sprang up across the continent.

Homely and simple though it was, the T was perfect for most people and most roads. Its three-point suspension could romp over hummocks like a loose-jointed boy. Its 13½ inch axle clearance swooped above the ruts. Its

A road scene near a beach in 1922. It is interesting to note that all but two or three of the cars are Fords.

vanadium-alloy steel components were strong beyond their weight. Its planetary transmission, though needing a page of explanatory diagrams, was so sensible that it became the mechanical basis for modern automatic transmissions.

Its radiator and lamps, originally brass, soon became no-nonsense black. Some of the first body styles were available in red, gray or green; from then until almost the end the T was black, take it or leave it. The tinny-looking body inspired awful jokes: Ford-joke farmer tears the tin roof off his barn and mails it to Ford; a week later the company writes: "Your Model T is the worst wreck we've ever seen; it will take us two weeks to fix it." But beneath that scrawny hide throbbed a motor that resisted shocking punishment. Dr. F. W. Andrews of Summerland, B.C. drove across Lake Okanagan and went through the ice. The doctor was badly shaken but his Ford, when fished out, ran fine.

An early Ford crossing the Nation River in Eastern Ontario by ferry.

Jokes to the contrary, the Model T was a pace-setter. It offered the first motor block cast as a single unit and the first removable cylinder head. It was one of the first cars anywhere with the steering wheel on the left side, although right-hand steering was still produced for those provinces that needed it. One advantage of left-hand drive was that two Ford drivers, gallumphing down some lonely road, could meet, pull up side by side and swap lies and motoring horror stories from their drivers' seats with the special camaraderie of T-men everywhere.

Starting and driving a T was an art and challenge. If a fool or a novice wrapped his thumb around the crank handle, the Lizzie usually kicked back and broke his arm. It was so hard to start on cold mornings that owners chanted a Lewis Carroll parody:

> Speak harshly to your little Ford,
>   And kick it when it freezes;
> It does it only to annoy,
>   Because it knows it teases.

Actually, there was an approved winter starting ritual, recalled by Elford Bell of Shamrock, Sask.

One of Calgary's earliest Model T Ford accidents, 1913.

"First you poured most of a kettle of boiling water into the radiator, saving some for the intake manifold," Elford remembers. "Then you jacked up the left rear wheel while the motor thawed out a little. The planetary transmission dragged so hard when cold that it was almost impossible to turn the motor without jacking a wheel and letting everything turn.

"Then a good solid hold on the permanently fastened crank with your right hand and the choke wire in your left hand, plus a few words of encouragement or otherwise, depending on your temper at the time, and it was surprising how rarely the old T failed to come right to life. You then let it warm before lowering the jack." When left warming by itself, a T sometimes slipped off its jack and ran around the yard.

The driving controls were no more complicated than, say, the controls of an Apollo XI. The T had a horizontal hand accelerator under the steering wheel, a vertical lever at the left hand, and three pedals. The right or "B" pedal operated the brake. The left or "C" pedal was the clutch. The center pedal operated reverse. As Ford's 1909 instruction book went on to explain, "The hand lever when thrown forward engages high speed; when pulled back operates the emergency brake. Hand lever is in neutral when almost vertical and clutch is in a released condition. Throwing the control lever forward engages the clutch in high speed; a light pressure on pedal 'C' throws in neutral; a full pressure on this pedal throws in low; a partial gradual release of the pedal again engages high speed." A wrong sequence of settings could cause the flivver to sneak away on its own while your head was turned.

But given half an understanding of the Model T, which was all most men could hope for, it was superb transportation. Cheap? Well, Dr. C. T. Ballantyne of Ottawa claimed he could run his "on a bottle of smelling salts." More specifically, he ran it 3622 miles during seven months at total expenses of $45.50, including 160 gallons of gas, 58 pints of oil, 6 flats, 1 new spark plug, $1.50 for damages incurred when running into a cart, and $1.00 to get pulled from a mud hole.

Pulled from a mud hole? For shame, Dr. Ballantyne! No Model T was ever stuck unless its driver erred. Alvy Robinson, a Woodstock commercial traveller, bragged that his 1910 T covered 48,400 miles in three years and "never had a rope on it yet." S. D. Jarvis, a T-man of the Hamilton district, used to earn pin money by hauling every other make of car up a steep hill near his home. Ford owners drove up-grade in the Rockies where other cars had to be winched by block and tackle. Ira Ribble, a Galt sheet-metal salesman, used to follow his farmer prospects out into the fields and woods. Timothy Craig Eaton, grandson of the department store founder, was driving his English tutor to the family's central Ontario cottage in the twenties when he realized he'd taken a wrong turn.

"The road's over there," he decided, peering through the bush. "I'll cut across."

"You *can't*!" cried the startled tutor.

"This is a *Ford*!" said Timothy Eaton proudly, and hippity-hopped through stumps and timber, back on course.

The all-time record for Model T capacity probably belonged to Ulric Leroux of Drummondville, Que., who in 1916 began giving fellow employees a lift to the local Aetna Chemical plant. More people kept piling into the five-passenger T every day until he was averaging fifteen a trip and once carried twenty-five.

Leroux was actually running a kind of jitney service. "Jitney," a slang expression for five-cent piece, came to mean the five-cent roving buses which caught on in cities all over this continent at the time of World War I, causing street railway monopolies to fight for their lives. Any car could be a jitney, but the cheap reliable Ford inspired the phenomenon.

In Vancouver, B.C. Electric reduced its fares to eight tickets for 25 cents, to meet competition; the city finally ruled that no five-passenger jitney could carry more than

The general manager of the London (Ont.) Public Utilities Commission invented the first automobile block heater for his Ford, which prompted a reporter to ask him why he had his car hitched to a tree. However, he was a bit ahead if his time, for heaters similar to this one did not come into common use in Canada until the 1950's.

In 1913 Mr. H. B. O'Neill and his family spent their two-week summer vacation driving in their Ford from Quebec to New York City—rather amazing when the roads of those days are considered. The two previous summers they had driven to Boston for their vacation.

eight people. In Edmonton the street railway began losing $5,000 a month while passengers flagged the quicker, more comfortable little buses. Winnipeg, when the jitney population rose to 800, ordered each jitney driver to register his hair and eye coloring, race, nationality and certificate of good character with the police. Other cities imposed high license fees. But for a while jitneys flourished despite official persecution because, as Goodyear Rubber Company's house organ said, in an eight-stanza poem of praise:

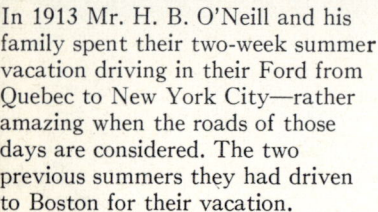

The O'Neills.

Air at thirty miles an hour
Forced in our lungs by engine power
Beats all the blamed physicians.
Good ozone plus a jitney bus
May make the railway magnates cuss
But heals our dispositions.

Meanwhile every commercial firm from the Hudson's Bay Company in Calgary to the Montreal Floral Exchange bought fleets of the Model T. City administrations everywhere used them. Between 1911 and 1913 Finlay McLeod of Toronto logged 80,000 miles carrying the Royal Mail in his Ford. The price kept going down (to an all-time low in 1925 of $395, plus $85 for an optional starter, plus $29 taxes) and people kept buying.

Youths took their flivvers into quiet pastures for wild joyful races. Old men tottered out for a last minute fling in the twilight of life; the four Briens of Wingham, Ont. (youngest: 74) said the Ford was their "greatest source of enjoyment." A Winnipeg baby, born in a Lizzie while the mother was en route to hospital, was named "Ford," naturally. Sheriff Calder of Saskatoon had seven flivvers for his force and said, "I don't give a hang for any other." Dawson City's first car arrived by riverboat in 1914 and "a majority of the population cheered wildly for the owner and the Ford." As a workhorse ambulance with Canadian forces in France, the Model T was affectionately dubbed The Jumping Bedstead.

Most important, the Model T finally wooed and won Canadian farmers. With pedal "C" pushed to the floor it could grind through mud or sand that would stop a horse and wagon. It hustled produce to market in half the time (C. P. Englestad of Corinne, Sask., built a chicken coop on the back of his). With rear wheel jacked up it would drive a saw, water pump, feed mill or would generate electricity. Charlie Meggs of Paris, Ont., saved his 1915 crop from the

Number One Police Station, Toronto, 1926. The car is a Model T, not equipped with radio.

Farmers were won over to cars when they discovered the many adaptations that could be made to help lighten the work load. Here, in Western Canada, a grain chopper is run by a car.

A 1922 Model T and an older car that had been made into a snowmobile.

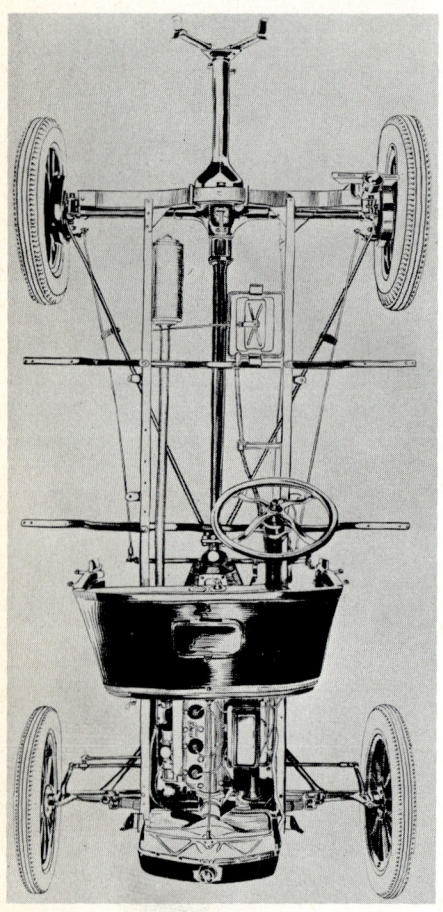

1926-7 Model T chassis. Chassis were available like this so that special bodies might be built on them, such as delivery vehicles or those used to promote products.

rain by working at night in the headlamp glow of his faithful Ford. It kept farm boys from drifting to the city (who needed girls or bright lights when you could play with a Ford?) and eased the loneliness of rural life. In 1917 farmers bought 60 per cent of the cars in Canada and the majority were the Model T.

While the car was changing Canadian society, Ford's plants and policies were revolutionizing the motor industry. Prior to World War I, a typical auto factory had long rows of auto frames side by side. Workmen moved from frame to frame, carrying their tools, adding parts and units from little stockpiles situated beside each frame. The men were constantly, inefficiently, on the move and always in each other's way.

Ford adapted techniques from the farm machinery and meat packing industries into his own unique chain reaction. Men first assembled sub-units in their various departments: rear axle, front axle, frame, motor, dash assembly, body assembly. "Each has his task to do and does it supremely well," glowed the 1914 Ford of Canada booklet. "Here we see a row of sturdy smiths, rough-straightening crank shafts and front axles, their clanging chorus augmented by the sound of a dozen swiftly turning emery wheels. . . . Here is a forest of moving belts, rows and rows of drills and lathes and an army of men. . . ."

Cutaway view of the 1926-7 Model T motor.

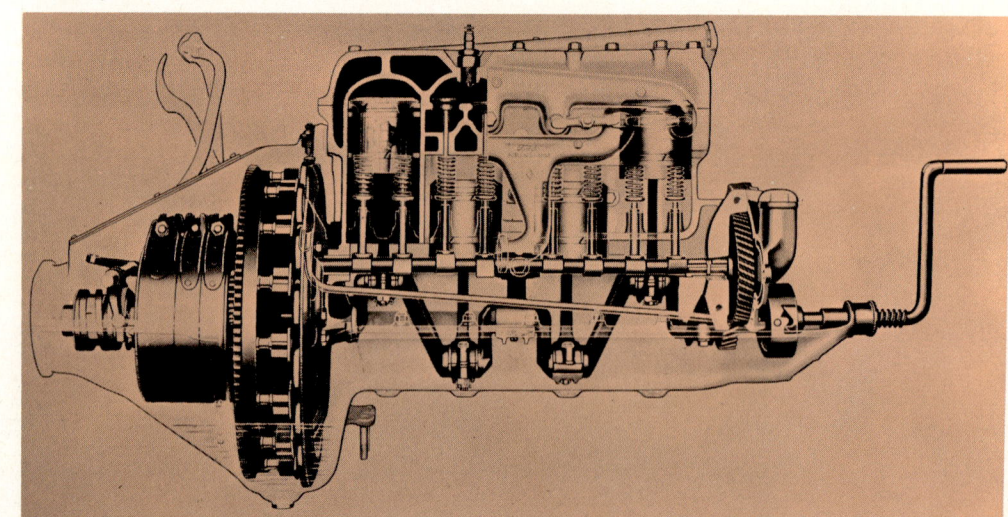

Next, each element of the T went on a power-driven moving conveyor platform past a series of workmen, each of whom added a specific part. Various assembly lines converged on a final platform where "it would surprise you to see how quickly these experts can assemble a car. Like Aladdin's magic castle, it grows from chaos to completeness before your eyes!"

When the finished Ford was ready to leave, dressed in black and full of gasoline, a tester jumped into the driver's seat. As the car rolled down a steep runway, he slipped it into gear and the stiff new motor cranked itself to life. It saved strained muscles and broken wrists—a typical Ford touch of ingenuity.

By the time other auto makers had copied Ford's assembly line he was ahead again, sharing the fruits of mass production with his workers and inspiring greater output. In 1915, Ford of Canada wages were raised to $4.00 a day and the working week was cut to forty-eight hours—about two hours per week less and $2.00 per day more than any rival's.

So the whole land praised Ford again. Canadians hummed the songs: *I Didn't Raise My Ford to Be a Jitney; The Love Story of The Packard and the Ford; The Little Ford Rambled Right Along* (there was this fellow in a big limousine, out there riding with his pretty little queen and the car broke down, and "just about that time along came Nord, And he rambled right along in his little old Ford; And he stole that Queen as his engine sang a song, And his little old Ford just rambled right along"). And when the ten millionth Model T rolled off the assembly lines a U.S. composer, Frederick Conover, wrote *Flivver Ten Million*, which was played by the Boston Symphony, with a Ford horn in its ranks.

Finally Ford overdid it. His insistence on building the same basic model began to backfire. The public demanded something fresh. Other makes, notably Chevrolet, forged ahead in sales. Ford finally countered with the Model A. When the last T came off the line it was number 15,456,868. Nobody cracked Model T jokes that day. It was like the death of an old friend.

This was the first moving production line, started in 1913. Prior to this parts were taken to the car instead of the car being taken to the parts.

Two views of the mechanized Ford production line in 1914. This speeding up of production created a problem in regard to painting the cars. Out of necessity Ford turned to the paint that had been used on the wheels, a fast drying Japan black, used exclusively until 1925.

A VARIETY OF FORDS:

1904 Model C.

1908 Model S roadster.

1915 Model T couplet.

1909 Model T touring.

Model T centre-door sedan.

1911-12 Model T commercial roadster.

1927 Model T sport roadster.

1920 Model T touring.

1915 Galt.

Court Myers of Hamilton with his 1922 Gray-Dort special touring.

1922 McLaughlin special six. On this model the first running boards and shock absorbers appeared.

1920 McLaughlin.

1919 Pierce-Arrow seven-passenger touring. Owned by Ronald Fawcett of Whitby.

1927 McLaughlin-Buick coupe.

1928 Plymouth sport coupe. Owned by E. Edwards, Toronto.

Colourful licence plates from the collection of General Motors, Oshawa.

Norman Hathaway in his 1929 Packard Super 8 sport phaeton.

Harley Neilson's beautiful 1928 Packard coupe.

Ralph Turner in his 1929 Bentley boat-tail speedster.

1929 Durant "depot-hack" or station wagon. Owned by Jack Morton, Toronto.

1931 Buick, model 90, straight eight-cylinder. Owned by Larry Norton, Oshawa.

Aubrey Marshall with his 1932 Horch convertible cabriolet. This car once belonged to the Nazi Party. Canada's collectors own many rare and unusual cars.

1935 Packard Super 8 convertible sedan. Owned by Donald Bullick, Toronto.

1934 Pierce-Arrow twelve-cylinder convertible. Owned by William Parker, Toronto.

5

THE CLOAK AND GOGGLE HEROES

Oh, what a late-show hero that F. V. Haney would have made! Lean-jawed as a young Burt Lancaster, steady-eyed as a Pa Cartwright, sparse of phrase as John Wayne at the Alamo, he peered out from the pages of a 1912 *Motoring Magazine* and told about his summer's drive across Canada. Any latter-day motorist, given such an adventure, would have dined out on it for life. Haney's English companion, J. W. Wilby, more or less *did*: two years later he turned his wide-eyed observations into a book. But Haney, after 4200 miles and seven weeks of mobile hell in a Reo touring car, dismissed it all with one final offhand line: "The engine was running as smooth as the purr of a contented kitten." But, of course! He was a typical 1912 Canadian motorist. Misery? You took it for granted. The important thing was: did the engine run?

The "fun," as Haney put it, began August 27 when he and Wilby dipped the Reo's rear wheels into the Atlantic at Halifax for a ceremonial start, then headed west. At Amherst they hired a "pilot," the first of many to guide them through the unmarked wilderness. The pilot ran out of gas and fell behind. Then the Reo ran dry but Haney discovered that "if I blew into the tank, then plugged the vent with a piece of match, I could get over the hills...."

Yonge Street, north of Toronto, in the early 1900's.

North of Toronto it took a team of horses, block and tackle and a subsequent day's repairs to recover from one sand hole. It took another six hours to cross a four-mile rock-strewn detour where Haney literally rebuilt the road. Between North Bay and Blind River they portaged by rail and tugboat; the trail simply vanished.

From the Sault to Winnipeg the pair travelled by boat and train, then slogged west through rain and gumbo, guided by a school inspector. By building the occasional corduroy road over alkali sloughs, dodging among ploughed fields and fences and wading knee-deep into water holes to pre-test their depth, they reached the Rockies. Wilby wrote, "We have neither signposts, milestones nor other landmarks. . . . The road soon showed signs of fickleness. It varied at every half mile. It lost its fence, then regained it. It lost its wheel ruts, then picked them up again. . . . A microscope then would have failed to find the road and the barbed wire and sun became our sole guide. . . ." Haney simply reported, "We made our way without difficulty." In the Crowsnest Pass, though, he dryly noted that "our pilot suggested a hinge in the center of the car to facilitate making some of the turns."

From Yahk to Kitchener, B.C., they drove the CPR track, being assured by the agent that if any trains came "he would tell the crew to look out for us." Then it took four hours to scale twelve miles of mountain trail with block and tackle. At Creston a local trapper led them ten miles over a swampy lake bed; "Ther's a way tuh go but yuh gotta know it," he explained. They crossed the Kootenay on a raft, took boat and train to Castlegar and drove among stumps and stones to Trail.

On the old Cariboo Trail the headlamps conked out so their pilot of the moment climbed on a fender with a lantern. Then he glanced down at the Fraser River, 200 feet directly under his dangling heels, and hastily changed fenders. By road, rail and ferry they finally reached

Roads or "trails" were equally bad in every part of Canada. Attempts are being made to pole this car out of the mud near Pigeon Lake, Ont.

Travel by rail, with flanged wheels on a car.

A tollgate south of Bradford, Ontario in the Holland Marsh area. Tollgates infuriated the motorists, especially when the roads charged for constantly deteriorated.

Alberni. What else impressed Haney, besides the purring motor? "Halifax air still in one front tire!" he exulted.

A minimum of flats and a maximum of miles—those were the measure of a good trip in that second decade of motoring. The automobile was no longer a national joke, no longer a rich man's indulgence or a lunatic's plaything. Nearly 40,000 Canadians had a car in 1912 and, by 1920, around 250,000.

In retrospect it might seem vaguely indecent that, during four of those years, while Canadians at home were frolicking with the motor car, a quarter million of their countrymen were dying in France. But the ugliness of World War I didn't really seep into the Canadian consciousness until it was nearly over. Until 1914, nobody had heard of poison gas, tanks, submarine raiders, bombers, flame throwers, land mines or hand grenades. On the eve of the war, Ottawa, Moose Jaw, Lethbridge, Halifax and Vancouver rang with speeches and cheers. Montreal crowds sang *La Marseillaise*. Toronto men snatched off their flag-bedecked hats and sang *God Save the King* and *Rule Britannia*.

The upbeat of patriotism lasted long after the gallant muddy men in tinpot helmets, wallowing in the trenches, knew there was no glory in twentieth-century war. Belatedly, the country caught on too, but still the war was very far away. So, in and around those years, life and the auto rolled on fairly normally at home.

These were the years of discovery. The things you could do with a motor car! In Montreal you could compete in an automobile "gymkhana" ("jolly good sport," English residents termed it) with relay races, obstacle races, spearing rings from uprights—all from moving cars.

If you were a drayman, you could double your cargo and halve your delivery time by putting a wagon box on a car chassis and making a thing called "truck," which with its open top and sides and bare wooden seats was exceedingly miserable in winter. On one thirty-mile truck trip, Torontonian Scotty Wallace's sandwich lunch froze so hard he had to thaw and eat it after he got home.

If you were Dr. R. McLaurin, head of the chemistry department at the University of Saskatchewan, you made a McLaughlin-Buick run on straw—simple prairie wheat straw. You burned the stuff in a nearly airtight compartment, caught the escaping gas in a vast bag anchored over the passengers' heads, fed it into the motor and bumbled along like a Zeppelin on wheels. It took about fifty pounds of straw to go fifteen miles, which was impractical even in wheat country. The gas bag also tended to pull you into ditches during strong crosswinds. But the contraption *worked*, and as farmers liked to remark around the general stores at night, it showed what a fellow could do with his education, if he put his mind to it.

If you were nineteen-year-old Henri Dandurand, son of Montreal's first car owner, you one-upped your father by building the world's first mobile home. In 1911 young Dandurand designed a twenty-nine-foot six-ton motorized Pullman car. It had stained glass windows, running water, flush toilet, kitchenette, ice box, twenty-one electric lights, mahogany interiors, silk damask drapes, sleeping space for twelve, telephones between every compartment and speedometers located where passengers could admire its top speed (28 mph). There was just one little problem: it was too heavy for the local bridges. It broke seven one Sunday afternoon, so the thirteen Dandurands and their friends spent most of their time circling Montreal island. By 1921 the bridges were strong enough for the monster to carry Canadian Good Roads Association convention delegates to Quebec City.

If you were not especially inventive but were physically tough—in other words, an ordinary vehicle owner—you went "touring," the reigning passion of the times. Couples, whole families, entire contingents of Canadians chugged off for days on end to picnic, camp, pop in on startled relatives or just explore some new and hazardous territory.

"It is the poetry of motion, the ideal mode of travelling," cried the *Calgary Herald*, of touring. And when Regina's auto club made its first tour, twenty miles to Lumsden in July, 1910, the *Leader Post* raved on for twelve inches:

A steam tractor in trouble.

The interior of the Dandurand Pullman Bus, designed by young Henri Dandurand in 1911. It was panelled with solid mahogany and had phones and signals in each compartment. The curtains and drapes alone cost $800. Holding twenty-six passengers with berths for ten, it had folding tables, a complete galley and running water.

The exterior of the Dandurand Pullman Bus. It was built from a three-ton Packard truck with a special body closely following a Pullman coach. M. Henri Dandurand, age 76, is still living in the Montreal area. He sadly recounts that due to a change in fortune, the Dandurand Bus, as well as his father's other interesting cars, had to be sold. The bus was used as a sort of taxi for awhile. The last time Dandurand saw his elegant Pullman it was lying in a field being used as a bee house. It has since disappeared.

This picture appeared in a 1914 *Canadian Motorist* with an article entitled "The Pleasure of Erecting Road Signs." In this article Doctor Perry E. Doolittle encourages motorists to help and says "the small boy at the circus never had a better time than some O.M.L. members on the road." This, possibly, was true.

Occasionally the motorist's trip was the idyllic one he imagined.

"It was certainly an exhilarating run, as car after car went swizzing along at a fine speed through fields of waving grain, swishing the long grass on the sides of the trail. . . . The sun came out and cast a benign smile over nature, raising the spirits of those who were fearing a storm. . . . The committee had arranged for a repair car which followed behind the party. . . ."

Touring originated with the pioneer American motorist, C. J. Glidden, who first caught Canada's eye with his 1904 drive across country on CPR tracks with a flanged-wheel auto (the railway insisted he fit his tour between scheduled train runs, and take along a two-man train crew in the car.) The next year Glidden launched an annual United States tour over a designated route. Manufacturers used it as a showcase for new models, but it was actually the beginning of sport car rallies. Drivers were scored for reaching each check point at the right time without mechanical trouble. By World War I, every motorist was a tourer, privately awarding himself points for every trip he survived.

By any modern standard, motoring was still utter madness. The rural folk, although friendlier, could not entirely be counted on. A carload of Calgarians, out on a foothills drive one March night in 1912, were suddenly surrounded by gun-toting cowpokes who shot a hole through the car roof and galloped, cackling triumphantly, into the night.

Winter driving was strictly for masochists. The only way to heat most cars was, as one manufacturer suggested, "Take out one of the floorboards and let the heat from the exhaust fill the skirt of your overcoat. The detachable boards should not be immediately over the flywheel or one may find oil thrown on one's boots." Anti-freeze was a primitive mixture of water and salt or glycerine and alcohol. At least one Winnipeg motorist fled his car in terror when the anti-freeze caught fire in the middle of Portage Avenue.

So touring was usually reserved for summer and those glorified cow-paths known as summer roads. You could

A portion of a page from the *Official Automobile Road Guide of Canada, 1912.*

	Towns.	Hotels.	Garages.
52.2	**Brockville**		**Brockville Atlas**
			St. Lawrence Garage

Straight course, close along the St. Lawrence River, with delightful scenery. Between Brockville and Prescott there are three toll-gates. Junction point for Ottawa, the Capital City of Canada.

64.4	**Prescott** (opposite Ogdensburg, N.Y., International Ferry.)
	Daniels' Hotel and Garage

Leaving here, the roads get worse, although they are not really bad until Cornwall is reached. Best plan to ship car from Prescott to Montreal. East of Prescott continue on King St., passing under railroad (65.2).

73.9	**Cardinal**

(On the right). Cross railroad and go direct ahead on main road, passing iron bridge on right.

gauge the amount of traffic over any thoroughfare by the wayside rubble of broken springs, ruined tires and discarded chassis parts. The slang phrase "Eat my dust" was literal fact. The only relief from dust was mud, and any amateur detective could reconstruct a motorist's movements by the brand of clay on his wheels. On muckier village streets it was common, although illegal, to run the right wheels along the boardwalk.

Rural trails were only beginning to be marked. Ontario was farthest ahead with 1,000 crude signs tacked to trees and telegraph poles by hard-working motor clubs. Road maps were almost nonexistent, but a navigator could read aloud from a motor club guide book while his driver steered through the great unknown. An Edmonton-Jasper trail guide read, in part, "Mile 17.5 Pembina Hill; sharp curve to the left at the top of the hill. Danger sign shows where this turn is. Considerable care should be taken in approaching the hill. Be sure no traffic is coming up before starting down. There is one turnout only, halfway down the hill where cars or teams can pass with ease. . . ."

Every organized touring band had its "pathfinder," like the scout who used to lead wagon trains into Blackfoot territory; a man who knew each hill, ditch, curve, rut and and rock. In July, 1911 one such superdriver successfully led twenty-five out of twenty-nine Calgarians to Banff in seven hours, even though rain had drenched the trail. Of the four dropouts who stupidly neglected to take chains, the *Calgary Herald* wrote severely, "There was very little sympathy expressed for them. An auto that starts on a trip like that should never attempt it without proper equipment."

What was proper equipment? How did a tourer outfit himself for the "fun"? It took a full day of preparation. Cars were better, true, but they still needed a tune-up before every distance trip. Grease cups had to be checked and refilled, especially if a heavy rain had cut the soap-base lubricant. Service stations were still scarce—Canada's first, a Vancouver Imperial Oil tank hooked to a kitchen hose, didn't appear until 1908. Some country stores sold gasoline by the can, but a wise traveller carried spare tins of fuel and water.

He also strapped on two spare tires, as many as seven inner tubes, pump, jack, raw-hide tire-bandage (to wrap around bruised casing), chains, tire repair kit (rubber patches, adhesive, sandpaper, a small vice, a tin of canned heat) and a set of nail pullers. The last, attached to the rear mudguard, sometimes managed to peel off horseshoe nails before they pierced the inner tube.

Charles Glidden (right) about to set out on the 1906 Glidden Tour. The tours contributed much to popular acceptance of this new mode of transportation.

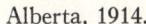

Alberta, 1914.

To this basic kit the tourer might add tow rope, block and tackle, lantern, and crowbar for easing stray rocks off the path. A fussy driver also took seat covers, headlamp covers for daytime driving, a canvas coverall to shield the car from overnight dew, another canvas to spread underneath where he could expect to spend several hours on any trip, and a collapsible rubber wash basin.

As zero hour approached, the tourer filled the radiator with filtered water, and strained gasoline through chamois cloth into the tank. Then it was time to dress. The men suited up in leather cap, goggles, pea jacket, duster (something like a butcher's cloth coat) and gauntlets. Raincoats, rubber boots and dust masks were optional. The women anchored their straw hats with cheesecloth auto veils, which also kept flying mud out of their mouths. They slipped into long-sleeve gloves and dusters down to the ankles of their $2.49 Dorothy Dodd high-button boots. Prudent ladies made sure their hems didn't dangle over the side or through the floorboards. One windy day in Watford, Ont., Mrs. D. A. Maxwell got her skirt caught in the chain drive of her husband's Maxmobile and was promptly stripped down to her knickers.

The men took the front seat, tight-lipped and courageous, wheel and guide book in hand. The women huddled in back, obedient, stoic and, ideally, blessed with strong kidneys. It was a long time between comfort stations.

If the tourers' luck was bad, a trip could ruin the family budget. Wayside food and lodging were cheap enough: a room in the Chateau Laurier went for $2.00, a dollar bought a delectable steak dinner at any Quebec inn, or the makings of a gourmet picnic with eggs at ten cents a dozen, butter at sixteen cents a pound and two choice roasting chickens for seventy-five cents.

But a new tire and tube for, say, a Packard 30 was $116. Gasoline by 1914 cost twenty-four cents in some cities; by 1920 it was close to forty cents a gallon everywhere. Ordinary motorists in most of Canada didn't have to be licensed until the twenties (Quebec was an exception) but cars did, and registration prices were rising. When John Craig Eaton bought Ontario License Number 1 for his 1903 Winton it was a simple $2.00 leather marker with an aluminum numeral. Alberta's first licensees paid only $3.00 and made their own plates: Joe Morriss of Edmonton hung a sawed-off broomhandle on his car, was charged with failing to display a license, and argued in court that the broomstick spelled out his number "1" (case dismissed).

By 1912, however, registration and proper plates cost $11.00 in Alberta and $10.00 in British Columbia. Ontarians and Quebeckers by 1915 paid up to $20.00 and $25.00.

The occasion of reciprocity in automobile licences between Ontario and New York State, May 19, 1916. On the stroke of twelve, flags were exchanged in the middle of the bridge at Niagara Falls. Doctor Perry E. Doolittle is seen in the Canadian car at the far left.

Tourists entering certain States had to buy their licenses, too: $3.00 in Michigan, $2.00 in Minnesota, $10.00 and up in New York. Canadian-American reciprocal licensing didn't begin until 1916 and wasn't complete until 1920.

There were other very real but intangible costs. Speed limits were creeping up: 15 mph in rural Quebec, New Brunswick and Nova Scotia; 20 mph in Ontario; 25 mph in British Columbia. But the new cars could muster up much more than that. "Going like sixty" was the synonym for ultimate speed, and it was an awful temptation to open her up on a lonely country road. Traffic fatalities began to make headlines and the non-motoring public screamed for action.

Suddenly the enemy was no longer a farmer with his do-it-yourself mud hole, but a cop skulking behind a tree

Mrs. H. B. Donovan, one of the first women in Toronto to obtain a driver's licence, and a friend, becomingly attired for a drive in her E.M.F., about 1909.

The first motorcycle squad of the Toronto police about 1910. They did not dress in uniform, in order to catch speeding motorists.

A 1903-04 licence plate, with metal letters on black leather.

with a stopwatch. In 1912 Toronto introduced a police motorcycle squad—four men on belt-driven Triumph bikes with orders to "Get those reckless drivers." Evidently nothing in the rules said the squad had to be uniformed, which accounted for the splendid box score of George "Sneaky Dick" Dickinson. Dressed in a natty business suit with a carnation in his button hole and stopwatch strapped on his wrist, Sneaky Dick lurked at measured spans of street. He clicked on the watch when a suspected speeder neared Point "A", shut it off when the car passed Point B, noted the license number, did his calculations by old math and notified offenders by phone. In eight years, Sneaky Dick averaged 10 arrests a week. The $10.00 to $30.00 fines represented a week's wages for most drivers.

Ontario provincial police also used and sometimes abused this primitive speed trap, coupled with the "fee" system. Until 1916 Ontario magistrates and constables were entitled to pocket a portion of all traffic fines, which one year totalled $15,572.

"Our friends the police sometimes too have oversights," grumbled *Canadian Motorist*, official publication of The Ontario Motor League, "such as seeing over the brow of a hill or around a curve, while their dollar watches with the press-the-button-stop attachment tell, or are supposed to tell, just how few seconds it took for the car to pass that telegraph pole around the bend in the turnpike. . . ."

In self-defense the OML and other clubs sent out booted, goggled "scouts" on motor bikes every weekend from May to November, spotting speed traps and waving **SLOW** signs at club members (identifiable by a beaver crest on their radiator caps).

Secretly, the motorists loved every minute of it. A matching of wits with the cops, a mechanical tussle with the

O.M.L. members were furious at the sometimes sneaky methods used by the police, so they sent out Road Scouts.

"A police outing" about 1913.

car, a test of skill and muscle on a slippery hill, the delicious uncertainty of navigation (would the "red barn," mentioned in a guide book as a marker point, have since been painted green or white?)—all of this was a supreme adventure; one of the last thrills left for a man. The only thing to top it, in 1914-18, was the privilege of going overseas for a shot at the Kaiser.

World War I was a singing kind of war, much more than any conflict since. *Tipperary*, *Mademoiselle from Armentieres*, *Pack Up Your Troubles*, *There's a Long Long Trail* —they came pouring out of the nastiness of the battlefields to become the folk music of a generation. But even the war didn't inspire as many tunes as motoring. Some 200 automobile songs tinkled out of Tin Pan Alley in those early decades and Canadians sang them all, the way we always sing American songs.

"Surely nothing like this coming of the automobile has every happened in the history of mankind," exclaimed the Toronto *Globe*. Nothing, indeed. Soon it would revolutionize the economy and living habits of North America. But for now, more than anything, it was a test of men. It molded contemporary heroes like Paul Welch.

Paul Welch, first man to drive from Edmonton to Calgary and back in a day! What was special about that? Only that in 1922, although eastern motoring was relatively sophisticated, the 414-mile Edmonton-Calgary round trip was still all dirt trail and right-angle turns, generally considered a three or four day journey.

Welch, the Edmonton service manager for McLaughlin-Buick, bragged he could do it in ten hours. This meant he couldn't slow down for anything, not even corners—a feat so obviously impossible that smart money came out against him in every pool hall and hotel lobby in Central Alberta. Let us witness this milestone in history.

It is 7:00 A.M., Sunday, November 5. Welch, thick-set with slickly combed hair, and his mechanic, Steve Playford, are poised in a McLaughlin-Buick Master Four at Whyte Avenue and 109 Street. His Honor Mayor Duggan heads the starting committee, a nice civic tribute to Welch. What a pity that Paul is going to make an ass of himself.

"Go!"

Welch is off—literally—in a cloud of dust. Suddenly the smart bettors, with a sick feeling in their wallets, realize

Paul Welch, "the fastest man of '22."

what Paul Welch is up to. The hell with *turning* corners: he is going to *slide through* them, the way Barney Oldfield did nearly twenty years before, the racing technique one day to be known as the "four wheel drift," an exacting manoeuvre for an average driver in a touring car on an Alberta 1922 road.

Welch is no average driver. At every corner, with a flurry of arms and legs, he jams his brakes, shifts down to low, skids into the turn, yanks the steering wheel hard over, floors the accelerator, up-shifts and roars on with no noticeable loss of speed.

Telephone and telegraph reports begin to trickle into Edmonton. Welch has made Leduc in $24\frac{1}{2}$ minutes. . . . He has made the 44-mile Innisfail-Carstairs stretch in 34 minutes . . . He is at Calgary city hall and it's only 11:32 A.M.!

Welch does not stay to sign the guest book or receive a set of city cufflinks. He shakes hands with a local alderman and the president of the board of trade, breathes hard for three minutes and heads north again. The wise bettors take hope. The road signs out of Calgary are a provincial disgrace: *so* confusing that Welch will surely end up off-course in Drumheller.

Nonsense! This is no novice at the wheel. He thunders north on the proper trail with police clearing the way through towns. Repair trucks are spotted at intervals but Welch doesn't need them. At 4:27 P.M. he reels over the finish line: a round trip in nine hours, 26 minutes, 55 seconds.

A cheering crowd shoe-horns him out of the McLaughlin-Buick (there is some concern that Paul will spend the rest of his life in a permanent crouch). He is reminded that he was testing a certain brand of shock absorber on this trip; how did they hold out?

"To tell the truth," Welch says, painfully honest, "they all fell off!" Later, when the manufacturer insists on a testimonial, Welch writes, still truthfully, that he would never *start out* on such a trip without this brand of shock absorber.

The broken shocks weren't important. For once even the car's performance was a secondary concern. The cheers and honors rightly belonged to the driver, Paul Welch, a mighty man like others of his time—durable, resilient, a motoring adventurer.

Freddy McCall, a famous racing driver of the late teens.

6

AN END TO INNOCENCE

Flamboyant though it was, the Paul Welch ride was really a relic of horseless carriage days. The age of derring-do was nearly over. By 1922 few motorists *had* to suffer—much. Motoring had reached adolescence: cocksure, awkwardly sophisticated, sensing the first real pleasures and chilly realities of growing up.

Roads were still universally awful but drivers had learned to live with them. No longer, at least, did they have to live with dusters, goggles and portable wash basins. By 1919 virtually every car was closed in, one of scores of improvements that everyone now took for granted.

Between 1920 and 1930 Canadian passenger auto registrations rose from 251,945 to 1,061,500. By the middle of the decade, Canada, with one car per fourteen persons, was second only to the United States in per capita ownership and third (after Great Britain) in total ownership. Ontario had almost half of the Canadian total; Quebec and Saskatchewan ran second and third.

The long trip was becoming commonplace. In May, 1923, when Fred Webb got home to Saskatoon in his Gray-Dort 19 B Special after a seven-month 16,621 mile jaunt through four provinces and twenty-three states he sounded as blasé as any 1970 tourist. He could only lamely tell the local *Saskatoon Star* that he "wouldn't have missed the trip for anything." No horror stories of major breakdowns or constant flats. The car was dependable transportation, and getting better all the time.

The twenties brought balloon tires, safety glass, tail lamps on both sides of the car, foot-control dimmer switch, back-up lights, adjustable front seat, gasoline gauge on instrument panel, ethyl gasoline, four-wheel hydraulic brakes, air cleaner, power windshield wiper, car radio and horn ring on steering wheels. Nickel-plated finish for lamps and radiators became standard. White-wall tires were a common option. Some models had a luggage trunk mounted lumpily on the back or side.

"The low-hung purring car today that clicks off 55 mph, or better, makes the massive high-built car of the early Teens seem almost archaic in comparison," wrote J. H. Boyd in the Toronto *Globe* of 1927. "Roads are better, cars are better, almost everything save the price of gasoline seems to be more attractive than in that era we often affectionately refer to as the good old days."

What Boyd meant about gasoline was that, along with inevitable price raises, several provinces were adding a gasoline tax: Alberta in 1922 with two cents, Manitoba a

year later with one; Ontario close behind with three. Taxes, fees and regulations of all kinds were closing in on drivers. Ontario replaced color codes with numbers to identify its highways. Toronto, in 1925, introduced traffic lights. British Columbia and the Maritimes abandoned driving to the left, which made motoring less like Russian roulette for visitors from other parts. Gradually all provinces demanded that drivers be licensed.

This in turn inspired the revolutionary idea that drivers should *practise* a little before going into active combat. Auto clubs introduced rudimentary driver training. In Edmonton, beginners worked out on Portage Avenue (later Kingsway), a concrete strip left stranded by the collapse of a real estate boom. Calgary learners took to the local fair grounds, which moved editor Bob Edwards to write in his *Calgary Eye-Opener*, "The auto club is building a special boulevard out on the prairie for the benefit of ladies learning to drive. It is two hundred yards wide and only one lady is to be allowed to use it at a time. The public will be excluded from these exhibitions. However, there is always the Medicine Hat Stampede to look forward to."

Highway speed limits, 25 or 30 mph in most places and far below the capabilities of cars, were bringing out the inherent nastiness and incompetence of the average driver. In Toronto alone in 1921 nearly 800 pedestrians were run down. By 1927 the Canadian Good Roads Association was pleading for a curb on "speed mania." The Ontario Motor League and Ontario Humane Society urged drivers not to carry dogs leashed on their running boards; at high speeds many had tumbled off and been strangled.

But speed, a dog on the running board, a hip flask and a flapper in the right-hand seat were the life style of the twenties—a style that depended on, was *nourished by*, the automobile. The country was seething, fidgeting with restless energy that was hard to define and harder to control. The slow old world was stirring with urgent matters.

Films and film stars were becoming idols and it was known, was *important* to know, which cars they drove and what they did in them. Babe Ruth played gustily on and off the diamond, and his battered moon face peered out from many a touring car. Lindbergh flew the Atlantic, solo, and his adoring public knew that Lucky Lindy drove a Packard.

The music changed from *la-lala-la* to *rickey-tick-rickey-tick*; the dances were suddenly all flying heels and rippling hips; the cars no longer hiccoughed down the road—they moved with a full-throated *Vroom*.

The most significant change in style and chassis was

At a convention of the Women's Institutes in Toronto in 1922 the president recited a poem, a portion of which was:
"Now Mary sits at motor wheel,
With skirts too short by half;
No lambkin stays her airy flight,
But you can see her calf."

Charles Lindbergh's 1927 Packard touring—now in a Canadian museum at Niagara Falls.

1937 La Salle convertible sedan, owned by Ralph Turner, Toronto.

among girls. As late as 1919 they'd been smothered in ankle length dresses over corsets and petticoats, long hair anchored with hatpins, legs encased in black or brown lisle. Now suddenly they were all short-haired, flat-chested, sipping cocktails, publicly smoking, with skirts so short you could see their garters when they clambered into a roadster ... OH, YOU KID!

Such a girl deserved more than a mere black flivver. Unless your father was totally without means, you tucked her into your Flying Cloud roadster, with her ugly best friend and your dull best friend crammed into the rumble seat, which was about the size and shape of a Volkswagen trunk. Better, if you could manage it, was a Stutz Bearcat, flaming red or yellow, very rakish; college girls were suckers for a Stutz. An older tiger—depending on how old and how well-heeled—might call for his date in a Pierce-Arrow, or an eight cylinder $11,600 Lincoln town car, or an EK Big Six seven passenger Studebaker with vanity case, smoking set, flower vase, heater and eight-day clock, all for under $3,000.

Certain other citizens . . . gentlemen with hat brims wide as beach umbrellas, acres of lapel and eyes as flat as yesterday's codfish . . . valued the Stude Big Six not so much for its vanity case and flower holder as for its ability, with back seat removed, to carry fifty gallon-jugs of booze. The dry hand of prohibition had fallen over the land.

America was totally dry. Canada was confused; it went into the twenties with total prohibition but, one by one, the provinces fell off the wagon until by 1930 only Prince Edward Island resolutely banned liquor. Even with prohibition in force, some provinces permitted distillers and brewers to manufacture for export overseas. So Canada became a bootlegger's paradise. A torrent of home-made and factory-brewed liquor flowed steadily, illegally, into the parched and grateful United States.

The only way for a bootlegger to travel was *fast*, generally by automobile. The accoutrements of his car depended on his level on the criminal organization chart. Al Capone, for instance, favored a $30,000 Cadillac with one-inch bullet-proof glass, befitting a man who was frequently shot at. Ordinary hoods fancied the Stude, or Whiskey Six, equipped with two spare tires, a 30-foot chain and a spotlight.

Its virtues were nowhere better demonstrated than in Manitoba. In a Winnipeg building laughingly known as the Blue Ribbon Oil Company, a group of earnest craftsmen brewed thousands of gallons of pure grain alcohol and pointed them toward that great but not-always-undefended border to the south. The whiskey followed various side roads to the vicinity of Piney, just inside the line. There it fell in a field, to be claimed by American drivers. If a jug or two fell in the customs officers' yards, it sometimes guaranteed an uneventful trip.

No matter, though; if the law *did* give chase the bootleggers' driver merely hunkered low over the wheel and coaxed the Whiskey Six to 80 mph while an accomplice threw out the chain, raising a mushroom cloud of prairie dust. If *that* didn't stop pursuers, the henchman focused his spotlight in their eyes, which usually put them in the ditch and made the bootleggers laugh so much they could hardly count their $200 fee.

Other Canadians were seeking their fortunes in a more legitimate but even more perilous way: making automobiles. The twenties saw the last gallant stand of the Canadian independent. A flurry of cars came out of Montreal: Forster, Parker, Duplex, Lavoie, Bourassa Six, Wright. Manitoba had a four-year fling with the Winnipeg (slogan: "As Good as the Wheat"). In Saskatoon the Derby, a sporty three-passenger coupe, sold for $1,750. But suddenly, almost overnight, the factory was abandoned, the principals were gone and some boys who later wandered

73

1923 Gray-Dort

1915 Gray-Dort touring.

1917 Gray-Dort cloverleaf roadster.

1920 Gray-Dort touring.

into the plant claimed to find a letter from an elderly shareholder pleading for her money back.

The La Marne of Trenton caused a buzz of excitement at the 1920 Canadian National Exhibition, and no wonder: it cost $3,000 and its eight-cylinder Hispano-Suiza aircraft engine could move the tubular-frame aluminum body like a juggernaut.

As well, there were established American brands: Ford, Chrysler, GM, Willys, Studebaker and Dodge. W. C. Durant, now out of General Motors forever but having one last shot at automaking under his own name, produced the Star and Durant in Leaside. In 1923 he also introduced the first production model station wagon—an open-sided wooden-bodied six-poster "especially suited for general farm use, city delivery, express service and station service for country resorts and estates."

The strongest Canadian bid came from Chatham, Ont., where the Grays, ex-carriage makers, moved into the twenties with their handsome popular Gray-Dort. Between 1915 and 1924 they marketed 26,000 cars, based on the U.S. Dort but with distinct Canadian touches. Gray-Dort offered some novelties over the years. Its Model 6 Fleur-de-Lys roadster had a rare seating arrangement: two front seats with a space between, through which the rear passenger squeezed into a cul-de-sac to ride alone—or with a friend if he wanted close company. The Grays would listen to any reasonable offer: one year they allowed a buyer $150 on a bay mare, taken as a trade-in.

Mostly, however, they confined themselves to quality manufacturing. Their 1922 19 B Special Touring model, for instance, was far ahead of its time with five disc wheels, nickel-plated radiator shell, motor driven horn, factory-installed front and rear bumpers, parking light, stop light and automatic back up. Within the mellow maroon body

The interior and exterior of the Brooks factory.

with black fenders were genuine Spanish leather upholstery and rear window silk curtains on a spring roller.

Then one day in 1921, a great year for Gray-Dort with 8,000 cars produced, the American, Josiah Dort, told Chatham's Robert Gray, "It's getting to be too much." The U.S. firm soon closed down. Gray-Dort eventually though reluctantly followed suit and thousands of owners genuinely grieved. This was a car with class.

About the same time the London Six was also dying, after three years in business. It was a good buy at $2,600: a choice of painted, cloth-covered or natural aluminum finish; eight-day clock; power tire pump; glass rear window. It could hit 70 mph, idle up Hamilton Mountain (which a contemporary Packard could not) or outrun the Windsor-Toronto train. The one thing it couldn't do was compete with the big-volume United States majors.

The Brooks Steamer of Stratford ran into the same Canadian economic stone wall, plus some problems of its own making. It was the only totally Canadian car at the time and, with the famous U.S. Stanley, the last steamer of consequence.

Early steamers had been frustrating, even in the years when *every* car drove its owner mad. Nearly seventy years after his father owned a Waltham, Montreal's first car, Henri Dandurand recalled its fickle disposition.

"She was so ticklish that she actually came from the factory with an expert to coax her," Dandurand remembered. "One of the big troubles was that you had to carry about sixteen gallons of water for the boiler and five or six gallons of gasoline for the burner."

The ninth Brooks made. Miss Jean Fleming says: "driven over 20,000 miles and still in perfect condition."

Oland J. Brooks.

With all tanks full the operator lit the primer, which lit the burners, which heated the boiler, which worked up a head of steam. "She smelled like the devil, she smoked and steamed and you had to watch the gauges," said Dandurand. "Father was like an organist, he had to play the gauges until they were just right. Then everybody got properly dressed and into the seat, said goodbye to the crowd, started up—and the damn steam would all blow out!"

By 1924 the steamer was less capricious. It could still blow a leak but this would not, contrary to rumors circulated by rival car makers, eject its occupants into the next county, although it certainly ended travelling for the day. On cold days it still took a half hour to get steam up, unless the pilot-light had been left on overnight. Yet the steamer had qualities that are endearing still: silence, a minimum of controls and mechanical parts, and no foul exhaust. It ambled down a street with a well-modulated hiss, or idled with a gentle *schussshh* like a contented dragon after a hearty meal.

To U.S. financier Oland J. Brooks, fresh from a stop in Toronto where he'd started a finance company, the steamer's hiss sounded like money. In industry-hungry Stratford, he bought an idle $55,000 thresher plant and the town eagerly took back a $50,000 mortgage. He created taxi companies in Toronto and Stratford, to interest the public in his steam car, got 125 men at work on production and another twenty in service stations and show rooms across the country. Brooks shrewdly planned to sell the car in the United States as well, thus avoiding the common Canadian pitfall.

"The Gentle Giant of Motion," as Brooks called it, had a leather-covered body, a twenty-one-gallon water tank and a fifteen-gallon gasoline-kerosene tank to fuel the burners.

"Wonder and amazement take possession of you when you sit behind the wheel and the smooth power of this

The Bennett buggy, named after Canada's Prime Minister of the early thirties.

A destitute family returning to Saskatoon from the north in 1934.

gentle giant of motion responds to the touch of your finger with a sureness that comforts your soul and gladdens your heart with its silent strength," said the Brooks catalogue. "The sensation of gratification is intensified to the point of positive exultation when the supreme mastery of the car is seen in the smooth and swift acceleration that enables it easily to leave all other cars behind after traffic halts. . . ."

Some former owners remember it differently. They say it couldn't keep up steam at 55 mph and had to be rested like an ageing horse. Also, the Brooks had only one plain chubby style which, at $3,885, took the steam out of many would-be buyers. Production wheezed to a halt in 1927. After three years shareholders were still screaming for their first dividends. In 1931 Brooks quietly paid off its last debts and disbanded.

There was no disgrace in its passing, or in the downfall of Gray-Dort, London Six and the rest. The twenties killed much bigger game in the United States: Maxwell, Overland, Jordan, Moon, Paige, Marmon, Chandler, Durant. The thirties wiped out Franklin, Cord, Reo, Auburn, Kissel, Pierce-Arrow, Stutz, Locomobile, Hupmobile, Peerless and perhaps the greatest of that golden age, Duesenberg.

Those cars the Depression didn't kill grew shabby, but their owners clung to them until the end. Families packed their pitiful belongings on the car roof, turned their backs on home and drove out looking for a new place, a new chance, any kind, to keep them alive. In the east they drove past breadlines and soup kitchens; on the prairie they pushed through choking dust and swarms of grasshoppers that turned a windshield into a sticky green smear. When the gas ran out or the car broke down beyond repair, they abandoned it—but with genuine sorrow.

Improvisation, invention, desperate ingenuity were characteristic of the thirties. A steady trickle of inventors pestered the Alberta Motor Association with ideas, such as a license plate light and a magnetized bar to pluck stray nails from the path of a vehicle—ideas they hoped would make them rich, ideas that *might* have caught on at any other time except this one, when the country was fighting for bare survival.

One invention spurned at the time—turn signals—came back to stay after World War II. But the most talked-about and wildly exciting idea turned out to be a total flop. In January, 1936 a Winnipegger, Charles N. Pogue, claimed to have developed a carburetor that would drive a car 200 miles on a gallon of gasoline. The news flashed through North America. Everyone *wanted* to believe it. Pogue's description (few people saw the actual model) was plausible: he said gasoline does not have enough time to vaporize completely in a motor; he had invented a preheating system that vaporized the fuel before it entered the cylinders.

He patented the idea, but after the first flush of publicity Pogue and his local backer grew secretive. In August he said his workshop had been burglarized and three test carburetors stolen. Rumors went out that the oil industry had "bought off" the inventor. The mystery lingered for years.

But when the patents expired, long after, no one picked them up. A University of Toronto authority on the internal combustion engine then studied all available evidence and pointed out that such a carburetor was literally impossible; it would mean that "about twice the amount of work energy can be obtained from a gallon of gasoline than is in it. This is equivalent to saying that you can pour about two pints out of a one-pint pot." Pogue refused to discuss the matter afterward. The best guess was that he'd honestly believed in the theory and had been as disappointed as everyone else. A man had to have dreams to hang onto in the thirties.

Which is why the Bennett buggy was such a comic-sad piece of improvisation—a defiant nose-thumbing at the Depression, a remembrance of good times past and a statement of faith in better times to come. It was named after Richard Bedford Bennett, who had the misfortune to be Canada's Prime Minister in the early thirties (and who, appropriately, hadn't driven a car since 1905, when he ran into a telegraph pole and swore off motoring for life). The Bennett buggy was a horse-drawn car body with wagon-tongue attached, engine removed. Wilbur Gwin in Saskatchewan took it a step farther: he trimmed it down to a fast, light two-wheel Bennett cart, which he usually rode standing up from a small rear platform, a 1935 Ben Hur on worn Dunlop tires.

It was the final indignity for the automobile, yet it was a triumph of the human spirit. People and cars came out of the thirties alive, tougher, plainer, grown-up. The years of innocence were over.

7

DR. DOOLITTLE AND THE LONG, LONG ROAD

The way Dr. Perry Ernest Doolittle was telling it to the *Calgary Herald* reporter, that September day in 1926, he might just have come back from afternoon tea instead of a nightmarish sixteen-day round trip to Vancouver. Yet there was no other way to tell it. Offhandedness was the indomitable Dr. Doolittle's style. Furthermore, every Canadian knew the nation's roads were atrocious and any traveller's horror story had to be exceptional to rate an audience. So when Doolittle said that the last leg of the trip, 271 miles through mountain snow a foot deep, was "not spectacular in any sense of the word," it was a factual report by 1926 standards.

Well, yes, he'd had to dodge a lot of falling rock. And get out to roll bigger rocks off the trail. And once his car was actually hung up on a boulder. Heavy rains had washed out the trail between Creston and Kiskinook, of course, and chains were "absolutely necessary." True, there was a place north of Spence's Bridge where "the road hangs midway on the almost perpendicular rocks of the left bank of the Thompson river. It is so narrow that only at certain spots can cars possibly pass. There is no parapet whatever. . . . At certain spots in this road where there is a sharp cleft in the rocks, the road is bridged by narrow wooden platforms. . . ." But all this, the doctor insisted, was "thrilling." Here was the *real* news: he'd come *through* the Rockies and only once had he resorted to ferryboat, over a sixty-five-mile span. Nobody had driven that much of the Canadian Rockies "on rubber" before.

Incredible news then, and equally incredible now, for quite opposite reasons. In 1926, a full twenty years after motor cars were commonplace, a Canadian still couldn't drive through the Rockies or the northwestern Ontario wilderness without taking to the railway tracks or a

Dr. Perry E. Doolittle

Perry E. Doolittle as a young cyclist.

United States detour. Not until after World War II did Brigadier R. A. Macfarlane and Kenneth MacGillivray win the Todd Medal, offered before World War I, for driving across Canada on rubber. Between that ten-day trip in 1946 and the beginnings of motoring, a lot of cars had slithered under the bridge.

At the turn of the century Canadian roads were so bad that even cyclists complained. They were mere horse trails: twisting, narrow, hilly and totally at the mercy of the elements. After rain they turned to fluid mud. After snow they were simply impassable, or packed into slippery slopes that sent cars skittering straight to the ditch. In dry weather they were shrouded in dust clouds or deep with sand.

In New Brunswick, the eighty-two-mile trip from St. Stephen to Saint John took ten to twelve hours in *good* weather. The approach to St. Johns, Quebec, was called *ventre-de-boeuf* ("beef's belly"): a liquid mess with a thin top crust that actually quivered for yards ahead when a man jumped up and down on it.

John Craig Eaton, one of Ontario's most ardent early drivers, once came home after a pleasant tour of New York State's paved roads. His good cheer dissolved north of St. Catharines; it took a day to drive the thirty-five miles to Hamilton. On the Hamilton-Toronto leg he finally abandoned the car in a sand trap. Out west, prairie gumbo was so adhesive, then and long after, that Dr. Doolittle's car once was solidly packed with mud from floorboards to wheels, on a trip near Edmonton. The vehicle had to be towed to dry land like a sled.

Slowly, governments, goaded on by motor clubs, began to act. Quebec built a ten-mile concrete road between Montreal and Ste. Rose in 1910. Manitoba began extensive use of gravel in 1909 and four years later asphalted a stretch south of Winnipeg. The new Toronto-Hamilton concrete highway of 1915 was a model for its time, and not a light-year too soon. A popular motoring rhyme of the day went, in part:

This was a typical rural road in Canada when the Canadian Good Roads Association was formed in 1914; (right) one way to get your Metz racer across a stream.

Roadbuilding gradually became more mechanized, but teams and wagons still played an important role.

> . . . But from somewhere east of Suez
> Where the roads are at their worst,
> Down to rocky Alabama
> Of the motorists accursed,
> For bumps and thrills and all the ills
> That, travelling, one gets onto
> The greatest jar you give your car
> Is Hamilton to Toronto.

Long before then, motorists had banded into provincial good roads associations. In 1914 the nation-wide Canadian Good Roads Association (commonly known as CGRA) was born in Montreal Arena, in air redolent with the leftovers from a recent horse show. It was prophetic; the CGRA was haunted by horse-and-buggy government thinking for years after.

Motor clubs and associations did their best while waiting for governments to catch up with the auto age. They offered cash prizes for road repairs, took civic officials on road inspection tours, oiled sections of trail at their own expense, put up road signs, published road guides, supplied split-log drags to farmers, constantly petitioned governments and tirelessly sought publicity. The Montreal auto club was lucky on the last count; in 1911 it took a batch of newsmen on an auto tour, got caught in a cloudburst and sank to the floorboards midway across the Laprairie Dyke road. There they all spent a miserable night. Press support increased noticeably thereafter.

All of these were stop-gap measures. Leaving the road work to farmers and rural municipalities, for instance, was erratic at best and sometimes worse than nothing. In Alberta one well-meaning amateur road-mender was seen patching a hole with the handiest available fill: nice sticky black loam. But gradually departments of highways emerged.

British Columbia was far ahead of others with a Department of Public Works to undertake highway building in 1908. Quebec set up a department in 1914; by the end of that decade most other provinces had one.

Suddenly everyone wanted to get on the good roads bandwagon. The Canada Highways Act of 1919 appropriated $20 million in federal money to assist provinces in construction of trunk roads; the objective: an interprovincial highway system. Saskatchewan's highways minister, S. J. Latta, somehow managed to relate good roads to love of King, hearth and mother. "How necessary a thing to the home today in Saskatchewan is a good highway," he told the 1920 CGRA convention. "And if we want to get at the essence of patriotism and make these people love their country today, we will have to get down to business and spend immense sums of money not only on railroads but good highways."

A year later the *Edmonton Journal* sent its own task force to Jasper by auto, pack horse and railway speeder. The *Journal* pathfinders left town in a great motorcade, with band music and crowds singing a *Journal*-composed fight-song to the tune of *Tipperary*:

> It's a short short way to Vancouver
> It's a shorter way for you
> By the nice new Jasper Highway
> If we only get it through. . . .

To Perry Doolittle, M.D., the growing wave of support was like a personal vote of thanks. For years he had been the leading advocate of a national road. In 1920, when he became president of the Canadian Automobile Association, a job he held the rest of his life, he'd been driving twenty-one years. Though medicine was his profession, he was a compulsive motorist, tinkerer and inventor. By 1908 he'd helped found the Toronto auto club, served as its first

Street paving with an early steam mixer.

Dr. Doolittle and his mother in a Stevens-Duryea. This photo was on a little calendar his son, Gordon Doolittle, made for his father in 1905. Right, Dr. Doolittle at one of his frequent roadside ceremonies.

president, and invented the Doolittle Demountable Rim for easier tire changing. It earned him some money (an English firm took a one-year option on it) but no fame (they dropped the option), which was the fate of all his inventions.

Yet Dr. Doolittle, like his fictional namesake, never stayed downhearted. The twenties were his vintage years, although he was then in his sixties. At any moment, any city or small town in Canada could expect to see "the genial doctor," as the press called him, bustling in from some god-awful motoring adventure, brimming with good humor and calling for better roads, more tourism, cleaner hotels and safer driving. His face looked out from every newspaper in the land: lean and alert, steel-rimmed spectacles, wiry hair parted in the middle and always, come sleet, flood or mud, an immaculate cravat, a high stiff collar rising like a snowbank around his throat and, usually, a stately black Homburg.

The automobile, said one newspaper, seemed to be "his permanent place of abode." He crossed Canada completely (subject to the usual detours) at last three times, and repeated parts of the trip on a half-dozen other occasions. Once he inched across a Quebec railway trestle, his wheels straddling the rails, with a 175-foot drop below. He loved to rise at dawn, drive a hundred miles before breakfast, and keep on until sundown. In his seventieth summer he drove from Winnipeg to Swift Current—more than 500 miles over less than ideal roads—in a day. Another time he left Toronto early for Montreal and arrived in such quick time and high spirits that he pushed on to Three Rivers, just for the hell of it.

Doolittle made driving look easy, which it was not, especially in the back country. Near Iroquois Falls, Frank Wood, later president of Ontario Motor League, was motoring home with his mother-in-law when he hit the grandfather of all bumps, which drove her head into the roof and demolished her $30.00 Easter bonnet. A year later, a couple of travellers got stuck on the Temagami-Cobalt road, tried to dig out, gave up, sat down and fell asleep. When they woke, their Chevrolet coupe had sunk out of sight. Eventually they recovered part of the top with pike poles. And in 1925 it took Doolittle and Edward Flickenger, a Ford of Canada photographer, forty days to drive across Canada, even travelling partly on rails with flanged wheels.

Nevertheless Doolittle made his point: If an elderly gent could drive across most of the country under existing conditions, how wonderful and relatively simple it would be to have a highway fit for everyone. It wasn't that simple. Although Doolittle said in 1932, a year before he died, "Everybody is getting behind the Trans Canada Highway," his dream was far from reality. Four years later the CGRA wailed in its annual report of "an 80 mph car with a 20 mph driver using a 35 mph road." Even when Macfarlane and MacGillivray made the 1946 cross country trip there was no highway worthy of the name.

The final nudge came in 1949, when Parliament passed the Trans Canada Highway act providing federal help for building the road, to be at least two lanes and twenty-four feet wide with ten foot gravel shoulders, curves of not more than three degrees, maximum grades of 6 per cent and a minimum stopping-sight distance of 600 feet in most places. Little by little the provinces, led by Saskatchewan in 1957, brought their roads up to par. Construction crews finally subdued the land east and north of Lake Superior. It took four years. Some equipment went in by barge and some by plane and helicopter. They blasted cuts through solid rock up to 600 feet long and 75 feet deep, and built 25 major bridges.

Out west the existing Big Bend highway—a notorious 190 miles of gravel, eleven years in the building to connect

Dr. Doolittle on the Pacific Coast, having symbolically dipped his wheels in the ocean.

A study in contrasts: (left) 1920 and (right) 1940 (Q.E.W.).

points only fifty-seven air miles apart—was replaced with the fine new Rogers Pass, shorter, wider, paved and shielded at critical points from rock and snow slides. When it officially opened in July, 1962, the Trans Canada Highway was complete.

Now the big road reaches 5,000 miles from St. John's to Victoria (not counting a few stretches of intervening water). Since World War II Canada has spent close to $20 billion on its road system, which totals a half million miles. There are individual masterpieces, such as Quebec's AutoRoutes and the 510-mile Macdonald-Cartier Freeway, commonly called 401. These are the main streets of Canada. Three million Ontarians live within ten miles of 401. More than 80 per cent of the country's industrial activity and 62 per cent of its population spread out from this super-highway's periphery. Professor E. G. Pleva, the University of Western Ontario's noted geographer, calls 401 "the most important single development changing the economic and social patterns of Ontario."

And why shouldn't a highway be an agent of social change? It serves the automobile, which is in itself an awesome influence on our lives; furthermore the modern highway is science at its best. This would have astonished Dr. Doolittle more than Trans Canada's completion: the roads which once lagged far behind automobiles in technical progress are now far *ahead*.

The highway engineer is a specialist. Colleges, led in 1956 by the University of Alberta, now offer postgraduate courses in every phase of highway engineering: design, construction, economics administration, planning. Economics? Indeed. What impact will a given road have on a community in terms of traffic diverted into or away from town, scenic views lost, revenue gained, noise and pollution nuisance for residents? What will it cost to light, repair and keep free of snow? How much traffic, and what kind, will pass over it?

Physically, a road is planned as carefully as a skyscraper. The route is chosen with the help of stereoscopic photos and ground surveys that include analyses of soil, rock and drainage. Pavement is not just pavement; the homely stuff called asphalt must be precisely mixed.

"In this country, there's no such thing as bad asphalt," says Dr. Norman McLeod of Imperial Oil, the nation's foremost asphalt expert. "Only badly-used asphalt." McLeod, who has devoted forty years to the subject, knows every detail of each of the eighty asphalts his company produces, thirty of which are used in road building. Road builders nowadays can choose from "conventional pavement" (part asphalt, part gravel), "deep strength pavement" (heavier on the asphalt) and "full depth" (all-asphalt, and tends to resist the tortures of sun and frost).

Even the machines of this new highway world are sophisticated: electronic devices that lay a surface smoother than any human could; bank indicators that detect a dangerously sloping grade; laboratory test machines that simulate the incessant pounding of traffic over a bridge.

And far from least is the science of making roads safe—safe despite the frailities, errors and incompetence of the average driver. What about dangerous guardrails with ends extending like spears at headlight level? Rebuild them to slope from the ground up, like a ramp. What of wayside posts and lamp standards that resist impact? Install the new snap-off kind that slow a runaway car but do not stop it head-on.

What *causes* accidents? This too is part of the science, engrossing entire safety organizations, and the highway men too. For years, the Ontario department has literally analyzed its roads, stretched them on the leather couch as it were, determining where accidents happen most often, and why. For a time Ontario employed a university psychologist as a part-time consultant. With two traffic engineers he pored over accident reports from serious trouble spots, analyzed what the road did to the driver, then recreated the driver's reactions. From this came recommendations and road improvements that saved lives.

Dr. Doolittle would have loved that super-scientific touch. It is creative motoring improvement at its best, as far in advance of its time as the Doolittle Demountable Rim.

Highway 401 at Avenue Road.

8

THE BUGS WITH DETACHABLE BRAINS

Early, early on a workday morning the sound begins to build over the tattered bits of city birdsong, half-rumble, half-roar, like some primordial beast yawning out of its cave. It is traffic, the first wave of 300,000 cars that will enter Metropolitan Toronto this day.

For the next few hours this city—and, to a degree, every Canadian city—fights for its life against traffic, with many of the trappings of actual war. Overhead, six radio station helicopters hover like dragonflies, rotors glittering, reports crackling back to earth from their traffic spotters (one is a lady in a *pink* helicopter, sometimes accompanied by a French poodle). Below, the Ontario Motor League's three reporters broadcast a steady stream of road, weather and traffic bulletins over nine regional stations—intelligence gleaned from the Ontario Provincial Police, Metropolitan Toronto Police and the OML's own five patrol cars spotted along major routes.

One of the CKEY helicopters over a busy stretch of highway near Toronto.

Metro Toronto's two million dollar traffic computer.

Metro police meanwhile have about 150 men on morning traffic duty: cops in yellow accident-squad cars, cops on motorcycles herding illegal parkers off the main routes, cops guiding car streams into major factory and office parking lots, cops unsnarling the instant congestion caused by an occasional traffic light failure.

The 880 traffic lights are governed by a $2 million computer complex on Jarvis Street, clicking, blinking, brooding over them. It is hooked to buried electric street coils that "sense" and report on traffic flow, helping mother computer decide which intersections must go red or green, and when. When the computer is working, it speeds traffic movement by 25 per cent over the bad old pre-computer days.

At crosswalks the school traffic patrols, suited up in peak hats and stop signs, regularly risk their lives to make the way safe for little children. No matter how skilfully they interrupt the river of cars, their presence fills the morning with screaming brakes and gnashing teeth. The crosswalk and crossing guard are part of the enemy: motorists are convinced of it.

The motorists! They come jostling in from 10, 20, 50 miles away, memories still raw from morning fights with their wives; ulcers and neuroses twitching from the debtors and crabgrass behind them and jobs they loathe in front of them; nerve-ends jangling as the traffic combat builds.

Some drive alone, solitary knights relishing secret thoughts, caressed by the mindless shouts of morning disc jockeys. Some drive in car pools, crowded among unwilling companions, secretly hating the others' daily company, jealously assessing their driving skills and errors.

They honk, curse, jockey for position into Metro. A dozen, on the average, have accidents after they enter the city limits. Ten per cent of the year's car crashes occur between 7:00 and 9:00 A.M. This whole mass movement teeters so precariously on the edge of chaos that one wrong glance, one malfunctioning traffic light, one hour of bad

The bumper-to-bumper "flow."

(Above) 1928 McLaughlin-Buick, owned by Bernice Marshall, Toronto. Made to order for the fall, 1927 visit of the Prince of Wales, it has a bar, a hand-rail for use during reviews and irreplaceable Lizard upholstery. McLaughlin-Buicks were a favourite of Edward VIII and he always had several on order. After his abdication he left Fort Belvedere for the English Channel and exile in his private car, a Buick limousine.

(Right) Rolls-Royce Silver Ghost hunting brake made for the Prince of Wales about 1912. It is now in the Antique Auto Museum, Niagara Falls.

(Bottom, left) The 1951 Chrysler New Yorker used for the Royal Tour of the Queen, then Princess Elizabeth, and Prince Philip, is owned by Frank Gordon of Toronto. It was for this car that Prince Philip designed a plastic top.

(Bottom, right) Larry Norton of Oshawa owns this 1939 Royal Tour McLaughlin-Buick. Hand-built throughout, the car is twenty feet long with a collapsible top of superfine duck seven inches higher than normal to accommodate the plumed headdresses of the royal party. This car was the last of the truly classic cars to be custom-crafted in Canada.

1968 Canadian Racing Champion Horst Kroll at the wheel of his Formula A Bosch Lola-Chevrolet at Mosport.

England's David Hobbs takes one of Mosport's challenging high speed bends driving his Formula A Surtees TS5-Chevrolet.

One of Canada's most promising hopes for success in international auto racing is George Eaton seen here in his Can-Am McLaren-Chevrolet at Mosport.

weather can cause monumental traffic jams or chain-reaction collisions that send a few to hospital and make thousands angrily late for work.

The survivors, those professional commuters with athletes' reflexes and carefully-mapped alternate "escape" routes down secret (they hope) side streets, penetrate the city core. They hand a dollar or two to a surly parking lot attendant or risk a $5.00 fine for overstaying one of the 7500 meters, then take the remains of their battered psyches to work—until evening, which reverses the rush and accounts for *30* per cent of the year's accidents.

To a civilized being from another galaxy, this twice-daily reflex action—scurry in, scurry out—would surely seem to be utter madness. Such a visitor, says U.S. economist Kenneth Boulding, would swear that Earth is inhabited by giant four-wheeled beetles with detachable brains. No such stranger could understand that many rush hour commuters would have it no other way. Studies have shown that, despite their savage complaints, many would never turn to a commuter bus or train, even if they could. Their daily ritual is a test of skill, a rare opportunity to be alone, a habit, a way of life.

A way of life. That, in essence, is the automobile in Canada. Commuting is only the visible tip of the iceberg, only a fragment of the car's enormous impact on every Canadian. It is the biggest single influence on our economic and social lives. If God ordained tonight that there would be no more motor cars, much of our economy and most of our pleasure would screech to a halt tomorrow.

Let's begin at the center, with auto making itself, and follow the ripples out. All figures here are, of necessity, approximate, because the Dominion Bureau of Statistics, the main and often the only source, is always woefully behind.

Canada, although by no means a major manufacturer of cars, nevertheless produces twice as many new automobiles per year as babies: about 721,000 versus 368,000. In actual per capita ownership we are Number 2, but trying harder. Our 7.7 million motor vehicles, of which more than six million are automobiles, work out to one for every 3.4 Canadians. This puts us behind the United States but way in front of Red China which, at last count, had one horseless carriage per 2,000 humans.

It also works out, in theory, to about one vehicle per Canadian household, although in fact more than a million households do not possess a car. Fortunately, another 755,000 right-thinking families have spared us from the world-wide humiliation of Red China by buying *two* or more cars. As for those laggards, those dropouts who have somehow resisted the siren song of the car commercial, the

The Highway 401-Spadina interchange. Even highways such as these are filled to capacity at rush hours.

seductive smirk of the used car salesman—they have not really escaped. Nobody escapes. The automobile touches every single life.

To begin with the obvious: more than 40,000 employees in motor vehicle manufacturing earn and spend around $300 million a year and make over $2 billion worth of products. Another 35,000 make motor vehicle parts and accessories, $1 billion worth, and take a $200 million payroll into the community. Still another 25,000—representing $2 billion in products, $200 million in wages—are in truck and trailer making, the manufacturing end of petroleum products and in the rubber business. There is no count of people in metal, glass and paint industries whose jobs depend on auto manufacture, or of the thousands in other aspects of the oil business. But they are part of the auto scene, as are the Canadian makers of 600,000 car radios produced each year. And, like all the others, they buy food, homes, clothes and services with the money they earn, directly or indirectly, by serving the automobile.

Manufacturing is only the first ripple. Beyond it are firms in retail sales and services connected to motoring: more than 5,000 new and used car dealers; 526 auto supply stores; 1,400 accessory, tire and battery shops; 6,000 garages; 3,000 paint and body shops; 452 car washes and 18,000 service stations, all doing in total millions of dollars worth of business. Canadian cars gulp about five billion gallons of gasoline in a year, and this is only part of the oil industry's stake. The more than 400 pounds of rubber and plastics in an automobile come chiefly from the petrochemical industry.

The ripples widen. Five thousand taxi companies; hundreds of parking lots; hundreds of car-orientated shopping centers with thousands of stores totalling $2 billion a year in retail sales; 250 or so drive-in theatres with

$17 million in receipts, including several millions worth of candy and soft drinks. And let us not forget the 190 driving schools, 287 auto and truck rental agencies, a thousand or more take-out food shops and the more than 6,000 motels, tourist cabins and camp grounds with their $20 million payrolls and their $160 million receipts.

Most of us would *like* to forget that biggest business of all—government—which flourishes and fattens on the automobile. Governments take in a billion dollars per year, 14 per cent of their income, in motor vehicle registrations and fuel taxes. The auto has spawned vast departments of highways, each with legions of employees. Ontario is blessed with *two*—Highways and Transport, each with certain functions related to motoring, so that a taxpayer seeking a simple piece of automobile information can be ping-ponged back and forth for hours.

Who can assess the effect on thousands of other kinds of Canadian shops, hotels and restaurants as we drive our 66 billion miles a year, sometimes dragging out 700,000 trailers behind us? Who has calculated the numbers, or the economic import, of auto insurance men, traffic policemen, road and bridge builders, sign makers, safety organizations, advertising agencies with car accounts—the list goes on and on.

The tyranny of the car—a tyranny we freely choose—extends into our homes. It dictates where and how we live. Sheltering it takes up an area equivalent to 13 per cent of the floor space of an average house. The car created suburbia and, now that suburbia is such a mess, is creating so-called "new towns": self-contained satellites complete with industry and services where, hopefully, people can live and work without the daily commuter war.

This will not stop us from *using* cars, of course. We will, say the market researchers, continue to buy beyond our needs and our means. Women will continue to be more practical car shoppers, attentive to safety, trunk space and parking ease, less dazzled by useless horsepower. And Canadian men will go right on impractically doing 88 per cent of the car buying.

Low income, or the basic needs of life, will not deter a family with its heart set on a car. True, new cars go to wealthier homes. Families in the $5,000-$10,000 annual income bracket account for half of new car sales; the over-$10,000 set, for another 40 per cent. However, three-quarters of the $3,000-$5,000 income group has a car and spends more per year on it than on clothing, furnishings, personal care, education, drinking or smoking. In every income group, car expenses rank third behind food and housing.

Low-income families, according to the Dominion Bureau

The snow plough with its sleek, forceful lines represents the expense and care that our roads receive.

of Statistics, spend about $400 a year on a car. That's rock-bottom expense. A *new* car, calculates the Ontario Motor League, will in its first three years of life cost $500-$1,000 in insurance, licensing, gas, oil, maintenance, parking and washing. That does *not* include any financing charges, or depreciation which over the first three years is a shocking 50 per cent of a car's value.

Inevitably, then, car expenses drag down those families who don't know how to keep out of debt. The Credit Counselling Service of Metropolitan Toronto cites the case of a young family of five with monthly income of $425 and debts totalling $4,234. Of this, $2,938 was owing on their car, and the monthly finance payments were running $186 —more than double what they could afford. They were persuaded to turn in the car.

Some people are merely financially crippled. Another 450 Canadians, on the average, are killed or injured in traffic each day—about one every three minutes. It is no consolation to know that we cannot, in honesty, blame the car. Most of the accident toll is due to human error: carelessness, lack of driving skill or such basic idiocy as failing to wear a seat belt when seat belts demonstrably save lives. Nor is it much comfort to know that the automobile and fuel industries are working harder at anti-pollution than any other segments of society, and claim they'll soon reduce automobile pollution by more than 90 per cent. Even an infinitesimal emission, multiplied by 300,000, can make a city unliveable during closed-in weather.

So the automobile kills, pollutes, brings on near-bankruptcy. Why do we love it so? Why did my next-door neighbor in one Toronto suburb, a wizened angry man who hated dogs and children, lovingly bathe his fat red car twice a week? Why do some men refuse to take their Oshawa/Oakville baby out on a winter day for fear of slush and salt on her pristine flanks? What's this infatuation we have for cars?

This question has fascinated every Pop Thinker and Sunday psychologist from Vance Packard to Marshall McLuhan and, incidentally, helped provide them with tidy incomes. Sooner or later, most relate it to sex. They have likened the car to a womb, a phallic symbol, a mechanical mistress. Toronto psychiatrist Dr. Daniel Cappon, with his sense of humor in overdrive, puts forward a good case for the car as an "extension of the bedroom," complete with symbols of embrace, erection and orgasm ("What if the engine is at the back? Sheer perversion!"). At least one sexual-psychological study was devoted to motorists' reactions while the gas pump nozzle was inserted in the gas tank: did they fidget, smile or sit transfixed? A Canadian author, taking refuge under the pseudonym

Michell Bedard, says women can predict a man's performance in bed by the kind of car he drives (watch out for the man who drives a Fury: he "is full of repressed rage and hostility because he was symbolically castrated by his mother early in life"). And a U.S. humorist predicts that someday we'll wrap up all this car/sex preoccupation by forming a Freud Motor Company.

But is it really a sex symbol? Or a status symbol? The status lines are blurring now. A number of behind-times company presidents and civic officials still bolster their egos with a black Cadillac, at considerable expense to shareholders and taxpayers, but in many circles the word "Caddie" is as distasteful as "Public Relations." A forward-thinking company president now chooses a Bentley, Rolls or, at least, a Lincoln. A number of well-heeled middle-age men are recapturing their youth in Mustangs, Corvettes and Cougars. Moreover, your modern college professor will foul the status lines by driving a rusty three-year-old Ford or Chev, a reverse-snob symbol. He knows he could buy or sell the average company middle-manager, and he knows *they* know.

On yet another level, the auto to a motor sport addict is a finely tuned piece of machinery, akin to a good horse or dancing partner. To a racing man, a car is speed, which is an end in itself. No one ever put it better than Sterling Moss: "To drive a really fine, balanced race car at ten-tenths of its absolute capacity, right on the edge, at the point at which one more mile will send it rocketing off the road into the woods—this is the most splendid and most rewarding sensuous pleasure, save one, known to man."

A 1966 "sourcebook of marketing and social-economic facts," *These Canadians*, came closest to exposing the motor car mystique. A man's auto, says this book, "is an extension of his ego; its power is his power. It makes him feel more substantial, more achieving, more masculine. Even a downtrodden male when speeding on the highway gets a sensation of being a rolling potentate. His car responds to every whim, something nobody else does. It enables him to rush forward and leave other people behind, to assert himself successfully. That is why men have the itch to buy a car at least one notch beyond what they can afford; that is why cars keep getting longer in length and higher in horsepower."

While this and all the other theories are maybe too esoteric or erotic for the average sweaty commuters, shoppers or vacationers, they know a car makes them feel good most of the time and, since they have to go *somehow*, this is the best way to go. Suburban housewives are desolate without it. A high school or college kid who can buy or borrow wheels would no more think of walking to school than crawling over broken bottles. Parking space is

In 1914 Canadians may have thought this ad an exaggeration, but the car is, and has truly been, "The Twentieth Century Idol."

a major problem, and the source of financial and aesthetic pain, at such outlying university campuses as U.B.C., Simon Fraser, York and the University of Manitoba.

"Few persons who have once owned a car give it up except in case of great necessity," wrote A. Currie, a University of Toronto economist, in 1967, "The psychological satisfactions of car ownership seem to outweigh the financial drawbacks."

So the automobile is the deity of our time, no better or worse than people make it. Dr. G. D. Campbell, director of technical services for the Canadian Good Roads Association, has predicted that motor cars will maintain their predominance for another twenty-five years. Yet to every *individual* car, as to every human, there comes an end, and it is sobering and somehow saddening to visit Industrial Metal of Canada Ltd., on the Toronto waterfront.

There among towering canyons of wrecked vehicles stands Bob, a hammer-mill so nicknamed by its operators, the biggest most modern auto-scrapper in the nation. It is an improvement on those huge metal presses that squash whole autos into tiny cubes, because Bob's twenty-eight mighty shredder rings, powered by a 3,000 h.p. motor, can chew up a car, separate its metals and spit them into tidy streams of steel, copper, aluminum, brass and zinc.

And how long does it take Bob to obliterate the Mechanical Bride, the Iron Mistress, Old Family Friend, the thing around which thousands of dollars and dozens of lives revolved for six or seven years? A little under thirty seconds.

The giant hammer-mill machine.

"Old Family Friend" on last trip.

FINE ART ON FOUR WHEELS

This handsome well-tailored man with the gray-touched wavy hair and the winter tan is not easily excited by rare or precious objects. He is Harley Neilson of Canada's chocolate and ice-cream Neilsons. He appreciates fine things; can afford them; *has* them.

But his Packards are special. They stir an emotion quite unlike his pleasure in the oil paintings, the living room tapestry, the music now pouring from one of the two grand pianos. He leads the way out of the elegant house in Toronto's super-exclusive Post Road district, past the three-car garage with Mercedes, convertible and station wagon, down a long walk to the four-car garage. There, behind one of his boats and a silvery Rolls-Royce . . .

Harley Neilson working on his 1928 Packard.

The original Neilson Packard in 1928.

Present 1928 Packard, body by Dietrich, being restored. Restoration took three years.

"Well," says Neilson, who is not given to fulsome statements, "there they are." Which in no way reveals how deeply he feels about them.

The 1930 phaeton is perfection, cherry red with a soft top, a classic, a regal ghost conjured up intact from forty years ago. But the 1928 coupe—well, now you sense a little of Harley Neilson's feelings, standing here, drinking in the sight for the thousandth time. It is such a *noble* car— lean proud caramel-colored aluminum body by Dietrich on a 143" wheelbase, straight-eight engine under the fold-up hood, nickel plate as thick as icing, two spare tires mounted like doughnuts at the rear, an actually *comfortable* rumble seat smelling gloriously of leather and with small leather flaps that fold out to keep unruly arms from marring either fender. Even before hearing its story, you understand why Harley Neilson loves this automobile.

When he was a teenager learning to drive, his father ordered this custom car's double, about $9,000 worth in 1928. It was an uncommon machine even then, but particularly special for Neilson. He grew from boy to man with the Packard-Dietrich. It was traded in 1934 but he never forgot it.

Years later he joined the growing army of 6,000 or so Canadian vintage car fanciers. Unlike some, he did not become a compulsive collector of *any* model. Like most, a car to him had to be somehow meaningful. He started, nostalgically, with a Model T Ford from the twenties. Then he heard that Al Capone's old armor-plated Cadillac was for sale in Blackpool. It tickled memories of the days when every front page screamed the latest infamy of Capone. He picked up the transatlantic phone, got the old wreck for $400, spent about $5,000 refurbishing it and later sold it to a car museum.

More and more he kept thinking about the family Packard-Dietrich. Two years of detective work—letters,

1924 Austin "Chummy," owned also by Mr. Neilson.

advertisements placed in small-town newspapers, prowls through garages—led him up to 1945 and the third owner. There the trail vanished.

Then Neilson got lucky. Through the Classic Car register, part of the car fanciers' vast international grapevine, he located an Arizona man with an exact duplicate of that Packard-Dietrich.

"With my heart in mouth I wrote him and as casually as possible asked him if it really looked like our old family car," Neilson says. "I sent along a picture."

He bought it for $950, had it hauled to Niagara Falls and drove it home—a pitiful rusted ruin that looked purely beautiful to Harley Neilson.

With professional help and thousands of dollars he spent two years repairing the running gear, rebuilding the motor, refurbishing the chrome, adjusting instruments, adding six new tires (exact replicas of the originals), relining the interior with imported English covert cloth—everything *precisely* as it was in 1928. He brooded over the color scheme for six months, then spent weeks sanding, lacquering, buffing, over and over, until the Packard-Dietrich glistened a creamy beige with brown fenders and trim, thin red decorative stripe and bright red wire wheels.

"They were to be as near to the colors of our family car as I could remember them," Neilson explains. "I guess I worried more about this detail than any other."

Now he drives the coupe to antique auto meets; though heavy on the steering, it is a pleasure to handle. It has won several prizes. Its value has appreciated. But Harley Neilson cherishes the car for another reason: it is a treasure from his past, and from Canada's.

"Some of us think these things are worth preserving," he says gently. "Summer nights I'm out washing and polishing it and people drive by, screech the brakes, back up and stare. And kids—they look at it the way I did when I was a boy."

Ten or fifteen years ago the passersby might have written off Neilson as an eccentric rich man. Now with vintage car clubs in every corner of Canada his is as reputable a pastime as art, china, coin or antique furniture collecting. Depending on the collector's nature it is a challenge, investment, recreation or simply a nostalgic excursion into the past. The thirty-eight Canadian clubs include housewives, truck drivers, bank clerks, salesmen and garage mechanics, many in their twenties and thirties.

It is no longer even mandatory for a member to collect cars. Many who haven't found the model they want, or can afford, gather automobile catalogues, emblems, stamps, sheet music, old novels based on cars, magazines, license plates or scale models.

1935 Packard, owned by Donald Bullick, Toronto.

1937 Cord, convertible victoria: supercharged, front wheel drive, V-8 engine, concealed headlamps. It was one of the first convertibles to have a rear seat. Owned by Mrs. Brian Brady, Toronto.

"Some of them even put the antique auto motif on their drapes, dinner plates, shirts and ties, or have their wives knit it into their sweaters!"

This is Peter Weatherhead speaking, with a visible wince. Weatherhead, an articulate young Toronto lawyer, wants public and governments to realize this is a serious, exacting craft as well as pleasurable hobby. "Otherwise some day we may not even be allowed on the road." To this end, on joining the club, he turned his first year into a "crash course on the old car movement." Now he pours out hours of his own time each week, gathering lore as archivist of the Ontario-based Antique and Classic Car Club of Canada (the country's biggest, with 1,200 members) and editing its magazine, *The Reflector*.

Weatherhead has no antique car, not for lack of funds (he has three late models) nor lack of interest (since age five he has collected catalogues, license plates, magazines and other memorabilia). He's put it off partly for lack of time, partly because, "I love them all. Every year has its great cars, its interesting cars." Weatherhead considers the automobile a genuine art form. Even its paraphernalia—lenses, stop lights, headlights, hub caps, gauges, signs,

1930 Model A Ford special coupe, owned by Hunter Robinson, Toronto.

posters, insignias—"could add a new dimension to our viewing."

Working artists are already applying these theories. Salvador Dali incorporated a touring car in one of his compositions. Automobile parts have been built into contemporary sculpture and mobiles. Montreal artist François Dallegret has won international acclaim for his series of "dream cars"—Astrological Automobiles, he calls them—based on the personality traits commonly associated with the twelve signs of the zodiac.

However, Peter Weatherhead needs no help from soothsayers or astrologers if and when he decides to go vintage. His first car will be a 1941 Packard-Darrin that he saw in a magazine advertisement as a child: "A beautiful piece of art." Nearly every other collector likewise sets out with a specific goal, usually the first automobile that made an impression on his life. Court Myers of Hamilton owns four Gray-Dorts because he courted his wife in that car. Robert Lane of Toronto owns a 1937 Chev: he learned to drive in it. C. F. Wheaton of Saskatoon "always wanted a Rolls-Royce, as long as I can remember," and getting it was the vintage car man's typical dogged pursuit.

So the scene now shifts to England where Wheaton, a sort of articulate Gary Cooper in a turtleneck, is on a business trip and, by the way, Rolls-shopping. He finds one he likes, discusses price, says "I'll take it," tells them how to deliver it and flies home. After a while he wonders (a) where's the car and (b) why nobody has asked for money?

The Rolls dealer in London has let it go. Well, you see, old man, you didn't come back with a deposit, so we

1923 Rolls-Royce tourer, 20 horsepower, owned by Roy Dodgson, Toronto.

1924 A.C. with the polished aluminum body and vee screen that was typical of sports models. Owned by Arnold Korne, Toronto. This car was judged to be the Best Vintage Sports Car at the 1969 *Concours d'Elegance* of the Antique and Classic Car Club of Canada, Toronto Branch. Below, a 1939 La Salle convertible coupe, also owned by Mr. Korne.

1934 Fraser-Nash sport roadster, owned by John Sebert, Toronto.

1935 Lagonda, drop-head coupe, owned by Kenneth Morrell, Toronto.

1913 Wolseley, owned by Frank Baillie, Oakville.

assumed.... Wheaton gears down through pained shock to mild rage. Inasmuch as he is an alderman, art collector and owner of his own electrical business, Saskatoon car dealers have never found it necessary to ask him for a deposit. Wheaton picks a car, they send a bill, he pays. Even so, if only the English had asked.... Wheaton has contacts in high places and after a while the Rolls man in London fervently wishes he *had* asked.

But Wheaton *wants* a Rolls so he goes to London again, quietly scouts the same dealership, sees one he loves, identifies himself, waits for the shock waves to subside, and closes the deal, *with* deposit. The Rolls arrives at Fort William. Wheaton flies to pick it up, and because it is past noon and he has to drive twenty hours before the following evening, in time to attend to some aldermanic duties in Saskatoon, he persuades customs officials to increase their usual slumberous pace.

Surely nothing else can go wrong? It can. On the road the Rolls blows a radiator hose. Wheaton limps into a service station somewhere in the wilderness and asks, knowing it is hopeless, "Got a rad hose to fit this?" Sometimes God smiles on the vintage car man. "Well, sure," says the filling station kid, and leads the way into a back room equipped with approximately all the radiator hoses in the world, including one that fits perfectly.

"This is it," says Wheaton, back home, working night after night, week after week, refinishing the Rolls to its original glory. "No more cars. This is all I want."

Tenacity, ingenuity, the ability to make decisions as fast as the board of directors of IBM—a vintage car hunter needs all these qualities. An Orillia collector finds a 1909

Tudhope sealed in an old chicken coop, blocked off by a tree. He cuts down the tree and plucks out the Tudhope by winch. John Campbell of Halifax is gassing up his 1961 Chev convertible at a filling station one day when, lo!, in drives a man in a '29 Chev coupe. Campbell eyes it greedily like a gourmet surveying an exquisite meal. He *must* have it. Yes, it's for sale (who'd want a '29 Chev if he could unload it?). How much? Well . . . the other man eyes Campbell's convertible . . . how about (chuckle) an even trade? Done! They settle it on the spot and Campbell drives away in a car which subsequently wins him several prizes, while the stranger with a glazed eye goes home in the convertible to tell his family about the live one he met today at the gas station.

The standing joke and secret dream of vintage car addicts is the garage or barn full of automobile treasures owned by a little apple-cheeked lady who has nearly forgotten them but will sell them cheap to a nice young man.

1935 Auburn convertible coupe, with Lycoming engine.

Such things do happen. "1908 McLaughlin was located in the basement of a house south of Montreal and was in fairly good condition when we found it. We had to demolish the basement wall to get the car out," says *The Reflector*. And, "1908 Sears—a close friend got stuck in a snow bank in eastern Ontario and asked a farmer to help him get out. In the barn was this car."

Gordon Edington of Toronto went out to buy an early one-cylinder Cadillac and found the makings of an exceedingly rare Canadian Queen scattered around the same garage. Ron Fawcett of Whitby, Ont., tracked a 1916 Chev to a Maple Lake, Ont., estate. Yes, said the widow, the car was in the barn; he could have it for $10. Fawcett pried open the door. No Chev. The widow was certain it had never been sold. Fawcett, about to give up, glanced at the roof. There wired to the rafters hung the Chev "like a black bat," crumbling but recoverable. Similarly, Bill McCurdy of Halifax found a McKay body strapped to the

1924 Vauxhall Wensum with swivel headlights. Owned by Aubrey Marshall, Toronto.

Ronald Fawcett on an Antique and Classic Car Club tour.

ceiling of a blacksmith shop, with enough other necessary parts scattered around. Charles Neville, of a Toronto construction company, followed up a chance remark by his next-door neighbor: her late grandfather collected cars and "never threw anything away." Back on the family farm Neville found an incredible cache of seven British Wolseleys, vintage 1911-1915, three McLaughlin-Buicks and a Maxwell.

These are the exceptions. Most rare cars still hidden around Canada are known to the serious collectors, but unavailable. Often, for instance, a widow locks up her husband's car after his death, and refuses to sell it for decades.

Most collectors therefore buy through dealers or other collectors, from advertisements in club newsletters, and with the aid of price lists such as that compiled by Saskatoon's S. M. Pask and P. B. Hertz with the help of an IBM computer.

What they must spend varies wildly with what they want. Price depends on the car's make, age, rarety and condition. The world is still blessed with many Model T Fords and a 1925 model, for instance, sells at around $500. Yet a 1912 Winton might cost $12,000; an early thirties Duesenberg, up to $30,000. A recent Pask-Hertz catalogue lists many cars in "fair condition" at $300-$1,000.

Although classifications may vary slightly among clubs, they generally fall into these categories: Antiques: anything up to 1929 except the classics; Classics: specified quality cars from 1925 to 1942 (such as Pierce Arrow, Cord and Auburn); general interest: 1930 to 1942, except classics. Ontario's Antique and Classic Car Club of Canada is the only club in the world to also recognize a "postwar

1931 Auburn 898 sedan. Owned by George Kershaw.

1932 La Salle restored by David Hill, Barrie, showing the tremendous amount of careful work that is done on a car to restore it to its original beauty.

thoroughbred" class: finest cars of their year from 1946 up to twelve years old. This is an effort to keep the postwar automobile from vanishing into the scrap heap, and to attract young members whose incomes or tastes keep them out of the vintage car class.

In any case, the purchase price isn't the final expense. Even the best-kept car will need work to bring it to competition standards. It must be indistinguishable from the original in every respect. The finish must be lacquered, not spray-painted, in the color used for that model and with every pin stripe accurate. Tires must be replicas. Nylon upholstery won't do. The only thing a competitor can get away with is modern metal in the engine's innards.

Restoring is therefore a long, exacting, expensive task. Ron Fawcett, who specializes in it, spent five years refurbishing a 1903 Cadillac. He is one of several Canadian experts who will sell a car ready-restored at prices of perhaps $3,500 and up. An individual can cut the cost by doing most of the work himself if he's a skilled mechanic, carpenter, upholsterer and painter. For people who aren't, Toronto technical school teacher and vintage Ford expert Paul Dodington now runs a night course in Model T restoration.

A do-it-yourselfer also needs work space, and few are permitted, as was a Ridgeway, Ont., man, to rebuild a

1902 Oldsmobile in the family living room. And finally the collector needs luck in his search for parts. An entire sub-industry has grown around the hobby, offering early model tires (at about $125 each), upholstery, tops, lamps, horns, generators, nearly everything for the commoner models. But to outfit an offbeat car the collector must hunt in junk yards, country stores, farm yards, small garages, homes that have old car lamps hung for porch lights or old wheels as gate markers. Car club newsletters cry out for "1931 Auburn dashboard with instruments" or "Two headlights and hood for a 1925 Model T."

When restoration is finished the product *might* be worth more than the owner put into it. Antique cars are increasingly, but not always properly, regarded as an investment. As more people flock into the hobby, some prices are going up. But novices have been stuck with ordinary old cars pawned off by unscrupulous dealers. As in the stock market, everything depends on what and how wisely you buy.

Experienced collectors discourage the investment approach. There are other rewards. For some it is the thrill of search and discovery. For others it is the creative challenge of bringing a wreck alive and perfect under their hands. For still others, it is the social pleasure of honking and chugging down the road in line on a sunny day while Mr. Average Businessman in his 1970 Chrysler gapes and wonders. For a few the glory of prizes is everything.

Perhaps the happiest, truest collector is of the Herman Smith variety. Smith, a big brisk man, self-employed, is in chemical sales, the toughest nitty-gritty kind of competition. He also loves cars, serves as archivist for Ford of Canada and has in his collection a Model C produced during Ford's earliest months in this country. Smith could groom his own cars for prizes, but he's not interested in *that* kind of competition. For him the hobby is refreshment for the soul, an appreciation of the problems and painful discoveries of early car makers, and a mental salute to their craftsmanship.

"When I come home and work on my cars," says Herman Smith, "it's as though I've stepped back into another age."

1931 McLaughlin-Buick. This magnificent car is the only Buick recognized as a classic by the Antique Car Club of America. It is an outstanding example of Canadian custom body building. It was designed by Winston Barron, Editor of Canadian Paramount News from 1931 to 1951. By the late forties he had gone over 500,000 miles in the car. The body is all aluminum except for the hood. Most metal parts in the car were specially cast in bronze. In the photo from the left: D. Watson (second owner), Winston Barron, R. S. McLaughlin, Norman Hathaway (third owner) and Ralph Turner.

10

"YOU NEED A LOT OF GUTS"

It is an awesome thing, this Lola T124 Formula A, crouched low in front of the pits at Ontario's Mosport Racing Park. It has a sort of brutal beauty, and the hint of enormous lurking power, as it waits here in silence. Perhaps someday, say in 1985 or 1990, we all will drive vehicles that resemble it; passenger car makers have always tagged along on racing car lines.

But this particular car was never meant for little old lady drivers, or most men for that matter. Its yellow fiberglas body, somewhat like a rocket, is slung between open wheels, just inches off the tarmac. The tapering snout has an airscoop and two stubby fins. Each rear tire is 14 inches wide. Behind, poking up like a miniature awning, is the "wing"—really an upside-down aerofoil. An aircraft wing gives a plane "lift"; this one, in reverse position on the Lola, holds the rear end down at high speed to give greater stability in braking and cornering. It cuts about three seconds off a lap on this track, which can win a race.

If the Lola is a trifle terrifying, the young driver is totally heroic. He is lean, hard-muscled and sun-browned with genuine modesty and a bleached-white smile. A beige uniform hugs his legs and ankles; red embroidery on the jacket announces that he is Horst Kroll. He slips on a crash helmet and lowers himself into the open cockpit. It is a mere slot, just big enough to admit a middle-size man, and he slides in like a pencil into a pocket: feet first, legs thrusting over the fire extinguisher and deep under the cowling to the clutch, brake and accelerator. The moulded seat embraces his upper body, in a half-leaning-back position. Waist and shoulder-belts buckled, goggles on, driving gloves on. Right and left side mirrors set. Horst Kroll flicks the starter and the Chevrolet 304 cubic inch 450 horsepower V-8 engine barks savagely behind his back. He pulls onto the track, smoothly but already very fast. . . . *zap*. . . . the first gear change. . . . *zap*. . . . *zap*. . . . the Lola raises its voice, a golden streak howling up, down, around Mosport's 2½ miles, blasting past the pits a minute and a half later. Horst Kroll, Canadian Driving Champion of 1968, is out for a little demonstration run during his 1969 schedule—and a handful of spectators are suddenly transformed.

There is an overpowering magic to this thing called motor sport. All of us yearn a little for it. Some manage to satisfy the urge with a Mustang or Firebird or another of the little pseudo-racing cars with snapping snarling names and more power than the average man ever needs or knows how to handle. Others by the thousands are weekend dragsters, stock car drivers, hill climb or rally competitors. And others simply watch, and dream private dreams in which they star in the most glamorous of the motor sports: racing.

If you are such a man on this autumn day at Mosport in 1969, you *are* Horst Kroll, with the wind flattening your nostrils and plucking at your lips; the track a blur beneath those open wheels; the Lola screaming proudly as you wind it up to 160 mph in the backstretch; the surge of power jamming your helmeted head back against the V-bar behind the cockpit. It is race day, any race day, and you are manipulating that tiny lever of a stick shift, up near your right hand, the way the man in the advertisements plays the Hammond organ. Your eyes flicker constantly from gauges to track to side view mirrors, watching the drivers ahead of you and those behind you, watching the corners you know by heart (number 2, for instance, sloping *away* from center, instead of *into* center as Mr. Average Motorist might expect; "Moss Corner," named after the great English champion, a nasty double curve that pulls plenty of drivers into the dirt, but you drift through it, four wheels sliding under control, for you are the Champion). You know that driving a racing car on this track is approximately like driving a passenger car on ice: at some point, which you will sense, the ultimate point in speed, tires will no longer adhere to asphalt. You must hang in there, just below that ultimate point. It is a magnificent, *alive* feeling. . . .

If you are a woman spectator, on the other hand, you ogle the handsome Kroll and enviously inspect his blonde wife, Hildegarde, gorgeous today in halter and flowered bell-bottoms, outwardly poised and serene. And there is her sunny three-year-old daughter, Brigit, who goes to the races and utterly adores her famous father.

Not merely Beautiful People, these Krolls, but The Beautiful Racing Family. Glamor, fame, the affluence of a champion! Lucky Horst Kroll!

Racing cars in Regina in 1921.

Well . . . . yes and no. The "luck" was earned and it was a long time coming.

The surface of international racing bobs with famous names and glittering records: Surtees, McLaren, Brabham, Hulme, Gurney, Hill. The list goes on and on. Much has been written of late about George Eaton, of the department store Eatons, who at twenty-three drives with flair and determination—finishing a race on a flat tire with sparks flying from the damaged rim; battling it out with Surtees for a final spot; placing third against top competition on a rain-slicked track. But the big-time winners almost invariably have sponsors or private means, or both. Eaton, while a promising driver who may someday bring international honors to Canada, can afford to fly to racing meets all over North America while members of his five-man crew bring one of his two McLarens to the scene.

Eighty per cent of Canadian drivers are not able to afford such amenities, certainly not at age twenty-three, yet they are total professionals. They have the qualities that Horst Kroll deems essential to a racing driver: "You have to be physically fit; your reflexes have to be out of this world. And you need to have a lot of guts." Guts not only on the track but in the endless years of financial gamble, with a family to feed and a bank manager snapping outside the door.

Many operate garages, sell racing equipment or hold down other jobs to stay solvent, and race with whatever resources they have because they purely love it. Given a few breaks, skill and some judgment, they parlay their effort into more wins, better cars and the all-important sponsorship that keeps drivers financially afloat. Many go broke. But among those steady pros who've made it, Horst Kroll is a model of skill and patience.

Ten years ago, newly arrived from Germany, Kroll could scarcely drive. He'd never owned a car, because he couldn't afford one. But at twenty-two he was an expert mechanic, with 4½ years' experience with Porsche, the German high temple of motor sport. In 1959 he started work with Volkswagen of Canada in Toronto, where "everybody was sport minded." He began serving as unpaid mechanic to a racing driver. One day, at the track, the driver complained that his car wasn't up to par. Kroll searched in vain for the trouble. The driver went out, and came back still complaining. "If you can't explain to me exactly what's wrong, I can't fix it," Kroll said. "Try it yourself," snapped the driver. Kroll did: "I wasn't even licensed. I turned my head the other way when I passed the pits so nobody would recognize me. But I did a few laps and I was *enjoying* myself. Suddenly they were waving me in. I was going faster than the regular driver, on a car that was supposed to be sick! I was making him look bad!"

Well, reasoned Kroll, why not combine driving and mechanics? Some of the world's top drivers were also excellent technical men; only such drivers can tell crews quickly and precisely how to fix an ailing car during a race. Kroll bought a Porsche 1600 because "I had great experience in fixing that car, cheaply." He began driving in 1960 and each year modified the engine or traded up to a better car. Gradually, almost imperceptibly, he began winning: Canadian and Ontario Hillclimb Champion from 1963 to 1966, two years Canadian and Ontario Formula Vee Champion, two years Ontario Race Organizers Overall Champion. By 1967 he was Canadian champion in his class (cars under two litres) and third-best driver in Canada.

He was now married ("I explained to my wife beforehand that I couldn't give up racing and if that upset her I would have to give up her!") and partner in a garage business with Walter Sabrowski, another first-class mechanic. Kroll was also establishing a reputation as a wise driver who kept his car in superb condition on a meagre budget—and who *finished* races. It's fine to finish first, but points are awarded *only* to finishers and as far down as sixth place. Kroll couldn't chase the more powerful cars but he frequently outlasted them.

Kroll is not the flamboyant "charging" type of driver; he can't afford possible damage to his car and, anyway, the mechanic in him hates to abuse a car. Of the 450 trophies he has won in ten years, one is a broken crankshaft he had mounted as a reminder of how a breakdown ruined a race.

Kroll loves to drive fast. He climbed out of his Lola at Mosport one day, saying wistfully, "If I only had the money for unlimited repairs, or a spare car, I could really give it the boot." In the qualifying runs before each race (wherein drivers are timed and accordingly given their positions in the starting grid), he always does a few fast laps to show the public that he *can* move, and in 1968 was fastest qualifier in his class on almost every occasion.

"But to me it is very important to finish without damage," Kroll says. "If somebody gave me a car and said 'Drive it very hard' it would hurt me! The Lola is limited to 7,000 rpm's but I like to keep it just under the limit."

In 1968 this technique paid off handsomely. He drove in 14 races with a six-year-old Kelly-Porsche and a total budget of $5,000 (some men spend $50,000 a year) and finished all of them. His 102 points in Canadian racing, 52 more than his nearest competitor, gave him the Canadian title, more cups for his shelves—but no money.

But for 1969 Canadian racing moved out of the bush leagues at last, with a $20,000 pot to be split among the top point-getters. Kroll also had some sponsorship from Bosch (Canada), famed for their spark plugs, Fiberglas of Canada and British Petroleum. He was also learning that he could finish in the money, although not yet the top money, in U.S. races (a sixth place in one U.S. race might pay him $1,200, whereas first place in a Canadian race paid as little as $300).

It was time for yet another, better car. In England he bought the best he could afford, the $13,500 Lola. As a Formula A car it was a single seater with on-board starter, open cockpit, open wheels with no part of the car projecting beyond the center lines of the wheels, two-wheel drive and a production engine under the five litre (305 cubic inch) limit.

He was still on a tight budget and a tough routine. He and Sabrowski drove to every race, taking turns at the wheel and sleeping in the truck (with the Lola on a trailer behind) on long distance trips. He still maintained his garage, and said the hard work helped keep him in shape.

"I swim and do a bit of running when I can. I don't smoke or drink. I go to bed early and get up early. You have to be fit, and you have to concentrate totally on the race, when you're out there. If you're going to be scared, you have no business racing."

Driving on a track, Kroll insists, is safer than on a freeway. At least on the track everyone is sober, knows how to drive and "we're all going in the same direction." Yet the threat of accident or death is always close. In late spring, 1969, Kroll's Lola lost its "wing" during a race and lurched wildly across the track before he fought it under control. In August, at the Harewood, Ont. meet, driver Al Pease accidentally rammed Kroll from behind. In the spectacular crash neither man was hurt but Pease lost a wheel and part of his rear suspension and had to retire. Kroll limped to the pits, had a ruined tire changed and the suspension hammered straight, manhandled the now-erratic Lola back in the race, and placed third.

Spectacular crash at Harewood. Kroll is in Number 37.

On race days Kroll likes to relax, totally, and forget the track until it is time to dress. If his daughter is along, he plays with her; "It's my best relaxation." But on the track he is all business, studying every inch of asphalt to see if it has changed since his last outing; analyzing every driver and anticipating his next move. "If I don't know the driver, I stay behind a few laps and study him and figure out how to take him. Then I make my move."

When the race is over he must make the long haul home and back to work, and to the incessant tuning and readying of the car for the next race. His wife, while never admitting to fright over her husband's headlong weekends, says discreetly, "I am always glad when he finishes a race." Such is the glamor of being a champion—the long grinding schedule, the constant strain to earn a dollar, the persistent danger of a crash that could wipe out a $13,500 investment, or even a life. But, yes, also the never-ending joy of speed, precision and competition.

By autumn, 1969, with the nine-race Canadian championship schedule nearly over, Kroll was fighting it out for first place with Toronto's Eppie Wietzes. Barring a disaster, he would finish first or second, with $6,000-$8,000 of prize money. At last the racing game was paying off.

"I want to drive as long as I can be competitive," Kroll says. "When I find I can't do a proper job anymore, I'll quit."

Right now, the man who never owned a car until 1960, is doing a very proper job indeed, as gutsy as the best of them.

Le Circuit Mont Tremblant in Quebec, where races of international stature take place.

11

A DRIVE INTO THE TWENTY-FIRST CENTURY

1. STOP AT RED LIGHT FOR SYSTEM-SCAN
2. INSERT CHARGEKARD
3. TELL EXIT POINT TO AUTOSPEAK

It is 2000 A.D. These instructions blink out at you from illuminated signs at the entrance ramps to AutoRoad, the new automated highway extending over what once were the Montreal-Quebec autoroute, Ontario's 401 and the Calgary-Edmonton highway—each a high-volume road between major communities where high density traffic made the enormous cost of AutoRoad feasible. The instructions are repeated in a woman's soft voice over the talk-box on your control panel, as are road, weather and safety messages throughout this trip.

You decelerate your bullet-shape turbine sports car, enjoying the rare feel of its power; so totally unlike the toy-car feeling of in-town electrics. But this car, like all combustion-fuel vehicles, is banned in the cities although its pollution rate is almost nil. A touch on the steering

Chevrolet's Astro III, turbine-powered three-wheeler.

A ⅜-scale model of Ford's Maxima, intended for jet thrust propulsion.

knob and you nose through an entrance lane to the light. A computer-scanner "reads" your vehicle for defects. (If any were found it would sound an alarm and order you into a service bay.) You slot-punch your charge card, which has replaced money in all the transactions of your life, and call your destination into the unmanned microphone.

In seconds the light turns green; your car's sensors lock onto AutoRoad; you fold your arms and enjoy the still novel experience of homing into the proper lane. Swiftly, silently (the turbines are almost noiseless), buried cables in AutoRoad lead you through Lane One (trucks: speed limit 99 mph), Lane Two (1998 models or older, 115 mph), Lane Three (conventional late-models: 130 mph) and into your own Lane Four at 150 mph. You lie back in the contoured seat to chat, read, watch television, until that gentle voice reminds you your exit is near and soon you will resume manual control. . . .

Fantasy? Not necessarily. All aspects of this little drama have been predicted in detail by appropriate experts. The only unknowns are whether such a system will, by early Century 21, be economically feasible—or whether it will be *obsolete*.

An eminent science writer, Arthur C. Clarke, whose predictions have been uncannily accurate, wrote in 1958 that a "characteristic road sign of the 1990s" will be "No Wheeled Vehicles on this Highway." By then, Clarke suggested, we'll be into the age of Ground Effect Machines, of which Hovercraft is one.

Nearly every other "futurist" (and hundreds of men in universities and major corporations around the world now bear such a title) expects most of us to still be on wheels by the end of this century. Although the GEMs of tomorrow may be quieter, more precise in their steering, less subject to wind blasts and create less of an air-blast tornado beneath them, compared to modern Hovercraft, they will likely share the drawbacks of such other aircraft as helicopters or Vertical Take-off and Landing craft: no workable traffic control or parking system for millions of people jockeying on short trips. It has taken seventy years for us to get a still-imperfect roads/controls/parking system for wheeled vehicles. A mass changeover to local aerial travel would be chaotic.

Before that happens we might well have a totally new kind of short-distance travel—something like Dick Tracy's "magnetic" air car, for instance. Anti-gravity research still preoccupies scientists, and it's been speculated that a breakthrough *could* come by mid-twenty-first century, or sooner.

Certainly by 2000 A.D. our audio/video/computer hookups between home, shops and offices will have eliminated much short tripping. Marshall McLuhan in *Understanding Media* implied that electronics would supplant the car in the nineteen-seventies. This was his only original pronouncement in an entire chapter on the automobile, and it's possible McLuhan was wrong. Decades hence we may still want to visit, shop or just flock out on the roads occasionally, partly to maintain human contact, partly because we like to propel ourselves in our own vehicles. It is a pleasure, almost an inherited reflex.

By then there will be forty million Canadians, with twenty million cars or more. Any family wishing to drive in both city and country will *have* to use two cars, both markedly different from anything now on the market.

Nearly half the people will live in and around two megalopolises embracing what are now Metropolitan Toronto and Greater Montreal. Another million will live in each of Edmonton, Calgary, Ottawa and Winnipeg; 2.2 million in the British Columbia lower mainland. In these cities the conventional car as we know it will be impractical in size and illegal in power plant. By the early seventies the gasoline automobile will be more than 90 per cent pollution-free. But the natural hysteria and wrong-headedness of civic authorities, plus the effort to eliminate *all* noise and pollutants from congested areas, plus higher combustion-fuel costs, will probably combine to drive the gasoline vehicle out. In mid-1969 it seemed likely Los Angeles would lead the way with just such a ban within five years.

In some city centres—assuming the major "city centre" concept survives in tomorrow's megalopolis, and is not replaced by a honeycomb of satellite centres—all surface vehicular traffic may be banned, in favor of underground rapid-transit and service pipelines and street conveyor-belt people-carriers resembling those now used in some airports.

More likely, though, surface traffic will be restricted to electrics, which will little resemble the Still or the

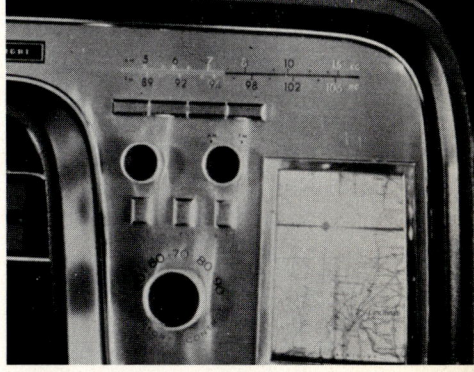

Ford's position indicator map which automatically orients with progress of the car (thus plotting the vehicle's position at any time), is a possibility for the near future.

Chrysler-Plymouth's parallelogram doors are ideal for tight parking situations.

Ivanhoe. They'll be small, totally functional battery-driven boxes with a range of 160-200 miles, ideal for commuting, shopping and suburban visiting. Gabriel Bouladon, a Swiss engineer and transport expert, foresees high-speed electric motors running at 35,000 rpm's, using alternating current without brushes or commutators, the wheels driven by a single gear ratio with an efficiency of over 95 per cent.

Each such "Elecar" will have just three instruments: voltmeter (the "fuel" gauge, monitoring battery voltage and reporting how much charge is left), ammeter (indicating the rate of fuel consumption and warning of any unduly high drain on current) and speedometer. City speed limits will probably still be about 30 mph but with fewer or no traffic lights and more multi-level intersections, it will be a *true* speed, unhampered by stop-and-go.

At night each electric owner will plug his car into an electric socket. By morning the batteries will be recharged. Some parking lots and curbs will have sockets for recharging at a price.

So far there's no economical electric but it's expected by about 1975. "A lot of people are saying there is a great public demand for the electric car," Dr. P. J. Stewart, of General Electric in Schenectady, told a Toronto scientists' meeting in 1969. "If we could find it, we'd build them." GE builds an experimental electric every few years. A recent 2,300-pound three-door model seated two children and two adults, could cruise at 55 mph, go about fifty miles on one charge and could have been manufactured in quantity at an estimated retail price of $3,500.

At least thirty other experimental electrics have been designed by industrial concerns in five countries, including most of the major United States auto makers. The major problem is still a low-cost power package to provide reasonably long range on a single charge. Silver-zinc, lithium and sodium-sulphur batteries provide up to fifteen times as much energy as the conventional lead-acid car battery. That still isn't good enough.

The fuel cell, a chemical converter known to every high school student, is a possible alternative. It turns fuel directly into electricity, as needed; oxygen and a hydrocarbon (such as hydrogen, alcohol or a petroleum derivative) react silently and without combustion.

The programmed highway is one approach to solving the problems of congestion and driver fatigue. The occupants, having selected their destination by computer card, relax. Spacing and speed would be automatically controlled.

An estimated 30 per cent of ground traffic in 2000 A.D. will still run on combustion fuels, but almost everything about those cars will be different: engine, controls, profile. A 1968 "Car of Tomorrow" exhibit in Washington included a far-out example: a nineteen-foot pushbutton dream car with seats that caressed the weary traveller, tires that lit up at night, an automatic electric shock for would-be thieves and the ability to drive itself or take orders by voice. The only thing wrong was the price—$75,000.

Back in the realm of possibility, cars will increasingly resemble aircraft profiles. Wind resistance at present highway speed cuts horsepower by as much as 50 per cent and increases gasoline consumption by 20 per cent. Seats will be moulded to the human form and, through air pressure, be made firm or soft to individual taste. If famed automotive and industrial designer Raymond Loewy has his way, future cars will discard waste space in doors, trunks and under fenders, or turn it into luggage or passenger space.

All major car makers have experimented with steering devices in their futuristic models. Over the years, one has had a streamlined version of the bar steering that Barney Oldfield used on his first racing cars; another employed a knob; a third had steering handgrips on each armrest of the driver's seat. One GM model had a central control knob accessible to both front seat passengers, so that either could drive. Pushing it forward accelerated the car; pulling it back slowed and braked; moving it to either side controlled the steering. Another model mounted all the dashboard controls, including steering knobs, on a pull-out console over the driver's lap, like an aircraft dinner tray.

Two experimental Fords—the Seattle-ite XXI and the Techna—illustrate other possibilities for the future. The Seattle-ite has four steerable front wheels for tracking, traction and braking efficiency and a separate engine compartment for either a fuel-cell electric motor unit or a nuclear unit.

The Techna has parallel hinged doors, structural glass windshield with no front corner posts, and hood and fenders that pivot forward in one piece for access to the engine. Instead of gear shift lever, it has a rotating ring which is wired to prevent doors or trunk from being opened while the car is in gear.

Both models have a computerized electronic information system with up to sixteen different kinds of messages flashed on a viewing screen (everything from coolant level and burned-out bulbs to weather conditions). In both cars the front seats are fixed but controls are moveable, with a power operated toeboard for brake and accelerator pedals.

Inevitably there'll be big changes under the hood. The

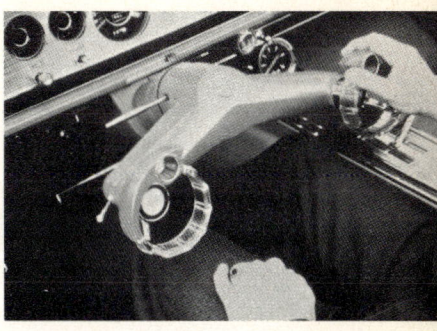

Ford's wrist-twist steering device is more comfortable for the driver and gives an unobstructed view of the instrument panel and the road.

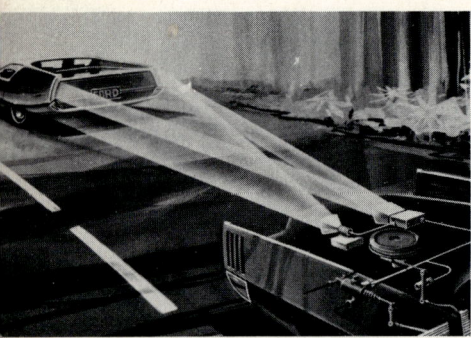

Automatic headway control is essentially a computerized brake-throttle control unit which is being evaluated by Ford in prototype form. When a car controlled by this device approaches another car from the rear, an optional beam is reflected back to an electronic processor that reads the signal and changes accelerator and brake settings to maintain a safe following distance.

gasoline engine, a dinosaur among machines, has improved but not really changed in more than 100 years. The pistons' wearing vibrating movement, and the one-firing-cycle-in-four is grossly wasteful. Ford engineers are experimenting with several improvements, some of which could increase fuel economy by 50 per cent.

A possible alternative is the rotary internal combustion engine—continuous power created by a circular motion. The turbine creates a similar effect. In one regenerative turbine developed by Chrysler, the intake air goes through a compressor, where its temperature reaches 435°. In a regenerator or heat exchanger, heat from the exhaust gases increases its temperature to 1,200°. The air then enters a firing chamber, is mixed with fuel vapor and fires at 1,700°. The escaping fuel-air gases expand and turn the turbine which turns the drive shaft. This particular model is simple (no valves, one spark plug, number of parts reduced by 80 per cent), quiet, vibration-free and air cooled.

Some experts say we will rarely or never drive our own cars in the future. Bouladon, the Swiss engineer, foresees cities with clusters of self-serve electric taxicabs spotted through residential and business areas, supply constantly geared to demand by computer. He thinks strikes, labor costs and their cumbersome nature will make buses obsolete by 1990. Others see an important role for buses. GM has explored "Metro-Mode," a system of express buses running on exclusive freeway lanes, like commuter trains. New York architects Craig Hodgetts and Lester Walker visualize a Landliner—an enormous high-speed rapid-transit train that would pluck up whole commuter buses and redeposit them as it sped non-stop through the linear-layout megalopolis of the future.

Assuming we choose to drive ourselves at least *some* of the time, the trick will be to eliminate driver strain and accident hazards as speeds increase. Bouladon visualizes an automatic highway, much as described at the beginning of the chapter. Several automobiles now offer a speed-control unit as an option; you can lock in any desired speed on a freeway and take your foot off the gas. Already, Ford is experimenting with Automatic Headway Control—a system of computer and infra-red transmitter that controls accelerator and brakes. When tied in with speed control, it automatically slows the car when it draws too close to another.

And why not, suggests designer Raymond Loewy, develop an electronic system which, when connected to a driver's body, detects impending drowsiness through his nervous system and sounds an alarm before he dozes off at the wheel? Better yet, suggests Lowey, science might devise a total warning system. This might be computer-controlled and based on the driver's individual characteristics and accident-proneness, the volume of traffic, day of week, time of day, road conditions, high-accident locations and similar factors. Then, for example, if after five hours of driving you approached Toronto in heavy traffic about dusk, the warning system would flash CAUTION-CAUTION-CAUTION, warning that you had reached your personal accident threshold.

Whether that ever comes, we'll almost certainly get the kind of oral warning system, coupled to existing traffic signs, described earlier in this chapter. At increasingly high speeds, conventional traffic signs register too late on our consciousness, if at all. They will be reinforced with warnings and information, beamed live or on tape from local broadcast points into each car receiving system. The same kind of system could carry bulletins of local scenic or historical interest.

A hundred years from now, maybe sooner, the thing called the "automobile" will be obsolete in every form. Some of the children born today will still be around, kept alive by a science that will have made death technically unnecessary. Some of them will dip into their video libraries for an amused look at those four-wheeled clumsy antiques of the twentieth century, trying to imagine the wonder, fear and outright hatred they generated. Some of those children and grandchildren of ours will electronically stimulate their own memory banks to recall the curious pride their fathers, every single one of them, even in the sophisticated sixties and seventies, felt when they took control of those machines, and commanded them to move, and usually were obeyed.

Off there in the future they will learn, or be reminded, that the automobile was imperfect, inefficient, a pollutant and a killer, often a financial disaster for individuals and whole companies. But they will also see that it was sometimes a delight; that it was a long step in the technological march of man; that it controlled the economy of entire nations; that it dominated a continent—no, *half the world*—for at least a century.

And perhaps they will remember that, in the days when the motor car ran, it was a great way to go.

THE CANADIAN CAR DIRECTORY

This chronology is by far the most comprehensive ever published, yet it can only serve as a stepping stone to more definitive future lists. Much of Canada's motoring history still lies hidden in the memories and family albums of individuals around the country. Names of obscure models and manufacturing efforts will continue to pop up as regularly after publication as they did before.

There'll be continuing arguments, too, over the definition of "Canadian" cars. The Earl, for example, a successor to the Briscoe, was sold here but manufactured only in Michigan. The Republic, often listed as a Canadian car, was marketed by the Republic Motor Co. of Canada in Toronto. This firm, affiliated with the Republic company of Hamilton, Ohio, was incorporated to manufacture, buy and sell automobiles but there is no evidence that it ever made one.

I found no evidence that the Beverly, Christie, Crosley and Cutting—included on some Canadian lists—were made here. Was a 1904 Austin produced in Toronto? Not according to city directories or government records. A Fulton truck was marketed in Canada but was there a Fulton car? Did Canada have a Carlson, Connor steamer, Black Diamond, Diamond Arrow, or McKinnon? Perhaps some reader will know.

And who knows about a Turnbull in Saint John, N.B. who allegedly built a car in 1851, or the 1899 Frost car of Owen Sound? Who can recall the names of the boys in Vienna, Ont., who in the 1850s or '60s built a horseless that ran the length of their barn, driven by a clockwork spring?

Until these are refuted or verified I prefer to list them only as leads or rumors. I have chosen also to set apart the outright U.S. models and to ignore the relative latecomers to Canadian car making. This is a list of *known* and *early* Canadian automobiles—and a remarkable record it was for a country then so young and undeveloped.

ACME

Acme Motor Carriage and Machinery Co. Ltd., Hamilton, 1910-12. Formed by merger of Hamilton's Baynes Carriage Co. and Goderich's American Road Machine Co. of Canada, with $800,000 capitalization. Directors included three Hamilton, two Goderich and two Detroit men. Its product was a 30 hp. touring car built "on the lines of one of the finest Detroit cars"; bodies made in Hamilton, mechanical parts in the U.S. By 1914 Acme was listed as a maker of "road machinery" only, in local directories.

ANHUT

Chatham, Ont., probably 1909 or 1910. A Detroit product created by a man named Mount, at a factory on Lacroix street near the old Grand Trunk tracks. Production probably limited to a few mockups. If this car was patterned on the U.S. Anhut, it was a six-cylinder overhead valve engine with two and four seater open chassis.

AMHERST 40

Two-in-One Company, Amherstburg, Ont., 1912. Seven-passenger touring car (first had right-hand drive) that could be quickly converted to pick-up truck by removing the rear seat section. Production probably limited to a half dozen or less. The first car was shown at the Canadian National Exhibition in Toronto in 1912, and subsequently hauled five passengers to Windsor, about twenty to twenty-five miles over bad roads, in forty-five minutes.

BARTLETT

Designed by R. C. Bartlett and built in Toronto, 1914-17. First seven had Northway engines; balance of about 200 had Le Roi engines. World War I necessitated seeking U.S. parts: Kelsey wheels, McCord radiator, Detroit Gear and Machine transmission, Detroit Gear and Axle axles, Allis-Chalmers electric system; frame by Britnell. U.S. entry in war ended parts supply and company operations. Deposits on 700 cars and salesmen's commissions had to be refunded. Two models: $665 roadster, $995 touring. The Bartlett had 28″ solid rubber tires, and four pneumatic rubber cushions instead of springs mounted between axles and body (last few cars had springs). Hudson Motor Company said to have offered Bartlett several million dollars for rights to rubber "air cushion ride" but war ended the deal.

BELCOURT STEAM BUGGY
See Chapter I.

BELL
Barrie Carriage Co. Ltd., Barrie, Ont. Incorporated in 1903 to build carriages, the firm by 1916 was making four-door touring cars and roadsters with bodies built in Barrie and four-cylinder Lycoming engines from the U.S. All business ceased about 1920. A "Barrie" automobile has also been attributed to this firm but neither company letterhead nor former employees verify it.

BENNETT
Essex, Ont., 1905. An out-of-town promoter named McKay visited Essex in 1905, obtained financial backing from the town to build automobiles, and set mechanic Albert Bennett to work on the first model. McKay left town before it was completed but Bennett, having more than $100 of his own money tied to the project, finished it. By Bennett's description it was "a poor thing" resembling the 1904 Oldsmobile and with a frame of $1\frac{1}{2}''$ angle iron that twisted whenever the vehicle hit a severe bump. Bennett drove the first and only model from Essex to Harrow and back at 15 mph, its one and only moment of glory.

BIRMINGHAM FLEXIBLE AXLE SIX
Birmingham Motors Corporation, Peterborough, Ont., about 1922. Probably based on U.S. Birmingham. Slogan: "The easiest riding car in the world." Continental Red Seal six-cylinder engine; Stromberg carburetor; Bijur starting and lighting; Gemmer steering gear; Exide battery, Jamestown radiator, Detroit Gear and Machine gearset; Timken roller bearings; New Process gear differential; Michelin disc wheels, special Birmingham frame by Sharon Pressed Steel Company; plywood laminated body covered with fabric, upholstering imported from A. Boyriven, France; springs of Birmingham design and special alloy; wheelbase, 124"; touring, 2000 lbs., sedan, 2500 lbs.; frame carried propellor shaft housing fastened by transverse members; only two oil cups, located on king pins; elsewhere, oil-less bushing used.

BOURASSA SIX
Montreal, 1926. H. E. Bourassa, talented mechanic, built a one-cylinder runabout in 1899; then a succession of larger cars to order, each different. Bourassa Six prototype had his own engine in Rickenbacker chassis; could not raise necessary capital for production.

122

BRISCOE

The Canadian Briscoe Motor Co., Ltd., Brockville, Ont., 1916. Based on French car already being made in U.S. Offered four-cylinder ($975) and eight-cylinder ($1,185) touring models and roadster ($825). Price included electric starter and lights, headlight dimmer, instrument board light, utility lamp and extension cord, top and dust cover, electric horn, robe rail, foot rest, speedometer. Cone clutch, 56″ wheel tread; 114″ wheelbase; 3 7/16″ bore, $5\frac{7}{8}$″ stroke, cantilever springs, floating rear axle, chrome-vanadium steel parts.

BROCK SIX

Brock Motors Ltd., Amherstburg, Ont., 1921. This firm was originally incorporated in 1920 as Stansell Motors Ltd., with Amherstburg manufacturer William Riley Stansell as a principal. The firm announced it would build a Canadian-designed five-passenger touring car with streamlined body, 118″ wheelbase, Warner transmission, Timken axles and bearings, 55 hp. Red Seal Continental engine, to sell for $2500. It's doubtful that this car was ever produced, although Stansell bought a factory, and Canadian car listings have made vague (and inaccurate) references to a "Standwell" vehicle.

By January 1921, the stockholders requested a name change to "Brock" (after the Canadian military hero of the War of 1812). Stansell was still a major shareholder but no longer head of the firm. In May, Brock Motors announced plans for the Brock Six, with 122″ wheelbase and extra-long springs. Presumably other specifications were close to Stansell's original car plans. By autumn the firm announced that, after some experiments, the first chassis was being moulded in an Orillia carriage shop. Brock Motors hoped to build 10,000 cars a year; in fact, it probably built only one. An accountant's report, years later, stated, "The whole business resulted in serious loss to everybody concerned."

BROCKVILLE ATLAS

Brockville Atlas Auto Company, Brockville, Ont., 1911-15. Included Models C, D, E, F and G, ranging from $1800 to $2400. Example: Model D—5 or 7 passenger, 40 hp.; dual magneto; optional electric starter; two electric headlights, two sidelights, one tail light; speedometer; license holder; mohair top with side curtain; electric horn; black with nickel trim and fine stripe; multiple disc clutch; sliding gear transmission, three forward and reverse; artillery type 35″ hickory wheels; front seat 49″ wide, rear, 54″, leather upholstery stuffed with horsehair. Right-hand steering. One of first to incorporate parking lights. Most parts imported from U.S.; body made in Brockville shops by Canada Carriage Company. Engines purchased from Atlas Engine Works, Indianapolis, Indiana. Transmissions from Warner Gear Co., Muncie, Indiana. One hundred motors and transmissions ordered in first lot.

BROOKS

Brooks Steam Motors Ltd., Stratford, Ont.; 1923-31; actual production, 1924-27. (See also Chapter 6). Founded by Oland J. Brooks. One model only (sedan), $3885; 3800 lbs. The 21-gallon 600-lb.-pressure boiler under hood produced enough steam for 450-500 miles; contained 484 flues welded top and bottom, and four miles of piano wire wound outside for protection. Fifteen gallon fuel tank fed burner, ignited by single spark plug. Two-cylinder double acting engine, similar to famous Stanley, and mounted on rear axle. Control lever under steering wheel operated throttle and main and pilot burners. Reverse was pedal-operated. Worm drive propelled rear wheels. Exhaust steam was led to turbine which drove fan behind radiator, which returned steam as water to the tank.

Metal body covered with "leather-fabric"; interior upholstery velvet plush. Throttle had tamper-proof lock in closed position. Water feed, fuel feed, lubrication, steam-pressure cutout at 600 lbs. and burner-extinguisher (when water level became abnormally low) all operated automatically.

CANADA

Canadian Motors Ltd., Galt, Ont., 1911. This car preceded the Galt (see below). The Canada Tourist ($1,575) was a five-passenger four-door model; 112" wheelbase; 34" wheels; water-cooled; multiple disc clutch in oil; sliding gear selective transmission with reverse and three forward speeds; foot accelerator; spark and throttle levers above wheel; speed changes by hand lever operating in an H-slot; emergency brake hand lever; speedometer, two gas headlights; lifetime guarantee. The Canada Roadster sold for $1,375.

CANADA BABY CAR

Canadian Baby Car Co., Montreal, 1914. Cyclecar came in three model names (Jap, De Luxe and Wizard), all two-cylinder air-cooled engines, 3.35" x 3.46"; Bosch ignition; carburetor optional (Schebler or B & B); two-speed planetary transmission; V-belt drive to rear wheels; 84" wheelbase; wire wheels with 28" x 2½" tires, semi-tandem; $495.

CANADIAN

Colonial Motors Ltd., Walkerville, Ont., 1921. Designed by former Packard man, E. G. Gunn. Slogan: "All Canadian car." Touring model, $2,600; V-type aluminum shell radiator with centrifugal pump and steel fan; TR Continental six-cylinder engine; independent front suspension consisting of two semi-elliptic transverse springs linked by short kingpin support arms at outer ends. Delco starting, lighting, ignition; Stromberg carburetor; vacuum feed fuel system and Stewart Warner tank; force feed lubrication. Single-disc clutch; three speeds forward and reverse; 120″ wheelbase.

CANADIAN STANDARD

Canadian Standard Auto and Tractor Company, Moose Jaw, Sask., 1912-18 (approx.). Company apparently went through two phases. In 1912 Moose Jaw trade commissioner Charles Brown visited a Fort Wayne, Indiana truck and tractor company; ordered complete materials for a number of cars, which were built and displayed. Then company officials disappeared. Three shareholders assumed control and employed Scottish mechanical expert John Robson to make a car for each of them: Cars were large handsome tourers with wire wheels, 132″ wheelbase, six-cylinder Continental engines, four speeds forward and reverse, body by Cadillac, Packard-style radiator. First car ran sixteen miles on a gallon at 45 mph, "so smooth and free from vibration a four-inch lead pencil would stand upright on the radiator cap," says Moose Jaw *Times Herald*. No commercial production.

CASE

Lethbridge Motor Car Co., Lethbridge, Alta., 1907. A contemporary U.S. motoring magazine listed this as a Canadian-made car, which is possible since the U.S. Case was not then being made. The Lethbridge Case Model A was an open five-passenger side-entrance tonneau model; 20-24 hp.; 4″ bore, 4″ stroke with four vertical cylinders; Universal carburetor; air-cooled; exhaust pressure feed oiler; side-chain drive; "any desired forward speed and reverse"; with the Worth system of disc and traction roller; change-gear control wheel on steering column; spark and throttle controls; dry cell batteries, jump spark, single coil and distributor; channel steel frame; 40″ front and 50″ rear springs, semi-elliptic; worm and segment steering; brakes on rear wheel drums and emergency brake by reversing transmission; 3½″ Fawkes airless tires; overall weight: 2000 lbs.; price: $2,000. Extent of production unknown.

CHATHAM

Chatham Motor Car Company, Chatham, Ont. 1906-09. Four-passenger open touring car; wooden body and upholstering by William Gray (later of Gray-Dort); wooden spoke wheels, right-hand steering; some four-cylinder water-cooled engines, some four-cylinder air-cooled Reeves engines. Between 75-100 produced. Financial difficulties in 1908 were briefly resolved by reorganization. Car was exhibited in 1908 Toronto auto show; won second prize in a Manitoba endurance test; carried Saskatchewan's J. B. Stauffer and family 3000 miles to Ontario via the U.S.

CLINTON

Clinton Motor Car Co. Ltd., Clinton, Ont., 1911-18. This firm grew out of the Clinton Thresher Company and included among its directors Thomas and William Jackson, Clinton manufacturers; Edward Cleghorn, who'd worked in motor companies in France, England and the U.S., and John Craig, formerly general superintendent of Canada Foundry Co. of Toronto and before that with Briscoe and Pierce Motor companies in the U.S. The company had shareholders in assorted corners of Canada, the U.S. and the British Isles, $100,000 capitalization and a factory that included power house, moulding shop, blacksmith shop, woodworking shop and machine shop.

The company, in its prospectus, predicted that the horse was "doomed to disappear from the scene" and saw the "necessity of a traction medium capable of transporting merchandise in larger quantities at a higher rate of speed which complies with the laws of sanitary science and retains all the elements of safety at a cost of maintenance vastly lower than was possible under the old conditions. . . ." In short, it proposed to make trucks in 1, 2, 3 and 5-ton sizes and "to handle some good popular priced pleasure car." It actually produced open trucks with chain drive, oil side lamps, blunt-nose radiator and solid rubber tires on spoked wheels. At the 1912 Toronto Auto Show the Clinton company displayed the "Clinton Combination", a 1200 lb. five-passenger four-cylinder open car ($985) that converted into a pickup truck. It also showed the Clinton Pleasure Car, a touring model.

COMET

Comet Motor Company, Montreal, 1906-08; first produced in 1907. Backed by Quebec businessmen. Open 4-5 passenger car, rear doors only, right-hand steering. Four-cylinder motor from Turin, Italy; 30-40 hp. (24 hp. French rating). Valves on opposite sides, mechanically operated. Cam shaft gears enclosed in oil tight case. Crank shaft fitted with five bearings. Simms-Bosch magneto and 4-volt 60-amp. storage battery, both controlled by single switch on dash. Hele-Shaw multiple disc-type clutch, running in oil; composed of twenty-six plates, alternately steel and bronze, each forming a small cone; throttle automatically closed when clutch pedal was depressed. Lubrication: pressure-fed oiler carrying oil to all principal bearings; grease cups and small oil cups for other friction points. Sliding gear transmission, four speeds forward and reverse, operated by one lever (with each change of gear clearly marked); direct drive on high; all shafts and gears chrome nickel steel; four ball bearings on main shaft in gear box, three ball bearings on counter shaft. Drive was propellor shaft to rear axle. French-made steel rear axle; Krupp steel extra heavy front axle with front wheels mounted on imported annular bearings. Frame of pressed nickel steel, dropped two inches forward of rear axle. Road clearance: 10″. Half elliptic spring (rear, 48″ long, front, 40″ long). Thirty-four inch wheels of second growth hickory, taking 34 x 4⅛″ tires. Large internal expanding brakes on rear wheels; powerful foot brake operating on transmission shaft. Wheelbase: 110″. Water-cooled, with American radiator. Gasoline gravity-fed to carburetor. Engine controls on quadrant above steering wheel operated throttle, magneto and timer. Aluminum body (sometimes fabric-covered); leather upholstery; dash, heel boards and all interior panels of mahogany trimmed with brass. Worm-and-sector-type steering gear; steering wheel of black vulcanized rubber on aluminum frame. Seven-inch mirror lens headlights with acetylene generator, oil-burning square side lamps, tail lamp, French horn, tool kit, rubber mats in front and rear, coat rail and foot rest in tonneau. Standard color: maroon. Carried a one-year guarantee. Total production estimated at 50-200 cars. At 1907 Montreal Auto Show, was priced at $5,000.

CROW

Canadian Crow Motor Co. Ltd., Mount Brydges, Ont., 1915-18. Associated with Crow-Elkhart company of Elkhart, Indiana. Production in 1916-17 of some 100 four-door touring cars and Cloverleaf Roadster; Lycoming engine; springs from Guelph Spring and Axle; tires from Goodyear and Dunlop; most other parts imported; bodies assembled and painted in small Mount Brydges factory. Firm went bankrupt in 1918.

DART

Dart Cyclecar Co., Toronto, 1913-15. Parts made in Detroit. Based on U.S. Scripps-Booth (which had a Spacke air-cooled V-twin engine, two-speed planetary transmission and leather belt drive).

DAVIS

Davis Dry Dock Co. Ltd., Kingston, Ont., 1924. John Davis turned from building pleasure boats to produce two touring cars, resembling contemporary Locomobile. Red Seal Continental engine, spoked wheels from Benjamin Wheel Company, axles and springs from Gananoque Spring and Axle Co., Timken rear assembly, frame by the builder. The first cost Davis $2-$3,000 to build and sold for about $900.

DERBY

Derby Motor Cars Limited, Saskatoon, 1924-26. Based on U.S. Davis, with probably only significant difference being price and nameplate. The latter cleverly had same first letter and same number of letters. President and general manager: L. M. Arsenault. Red Seal Continental six-cylinder motor, Ross cam-and-lever steering, Delco electrical equipment, Lockheed four-wheel hydraulic brakes, Duco finish, three speeds forward and a reverse, 110″ wheelbase, Tillotson carburetor. Models included: Series 92 —touring phaeton ($1995), Man-o-war roadster ($2100), Legionaire touring ($2150), 4-door sedan ($2450); Series 93 —4-door sedan, 3-passenger coupe, and 5-passenger touring (all $1750). Slogan: "Built of the best." A "few hundred" reportedly sold before plant closed in 1926.

DICKSON/FETHERSTONHAUGH ELECTRIC

One model made in 1893 for lawyer Frederick Barnard Fetherstonhaugh (reportedly to his design) by Dickson's Carriage Works, Toronto. Chain drive, wire wheels, tiller, "controller" (speed control and power unit), 15 mph top speed, fourteen miles on a charge. Motor and batteries designed by W. J. Still, Toronto. Initially had "fifth wheel" steering gear like a buggy; later was fitted with knuckle joints. Fetherstonhaugh drove it fifteen years.

DOHERTY

Sarnia, Ont., 1897. Stove manufacturer Thomas Doherty built two vehicles; the first was powered by a coil spring on the rear axle; the second used his own design of two-cylinder gasoline engine.

DOMINION

Dominion Motors Ltd., Walkerville, Ont., 1910-11. Firm incorporated with $150,000 capital to build four-cylinder 35 hp. Royal Windsor, similar to U.S. Windsor. Then reorganized and renamed Dominion. Designed by E. W. Winans; four-cylinder, 32-35 hp., 50 mph, cone clutch, straight line shaft drive, sliding selective type transmission with three forward and one reverse, 34 x 4" spoked wheels with rubber tires, I-beam front axle, semi-floating rear axle. Was shown at 1910 Canadian National Exhibition. Company liquidated in 1911.

DOMINION

Dominion Motor Car Co., Coldbrook, N.B., took over the Maritime Motor Company; produced a few prototypes in 1914.

DUPLEX

United Iron Works Company, Montreal, 1923; four-cylinder car on a Hudson chassis with two pistons per cylinder. Sedan priced at $1750.

FALCON

Gove Motor Car Co., Tilbury and Thorold, Ont., 1921. Set up by U.S. company to manufacture Falcon Light Six. Extent of production unknown.

FLEETWOOD KNIGHT

Single model built in Kingston, 1924, by L. J. Davis. No connection with the "Davis" car.

The Fleetwood had a six-cylinder sleeve-valve 80 hp. engine with $3\frac{3}{8}$" bore and $4\frac{1}{2}$" stroke; Stromberg carburetor; Delco ignition, starting and generator; Borg and Beck dry plate clutch; three-speed transmission: Spicer propellor shaft with two universal joints; Eaton axles; internal expanding service brakes on four wheels, and contracting emergency brake acting on propellor shaft and drum; five-spoke steel artillery type wheels with balloon tires on 20" rims; 133" wheelbase; sedan.

FORSTER

Forster Manufacturing Co., Montreal, 1920-22. Assembled in Montreal with Herschell-Spillman six-cylinder engine, right-hand drive, streamlined body, Borg and Beck clutch, Covert three-speed transmission, Timken axle, Eisemann magneto, Westinghouse lighting and starting, Temme springs, 125" wheelbase, Zenith $1\frac{1}{4}$" carburetor; wooden wheels, 33 x 4"; three-passenger coupe, five-passenger sedan, seven-passenger limousine.

FRONTENAC

Dominion Motors, Ltd., Toronto, 1931-33. Firm had latterly built Star and Durant.

Frontenac Six came as a sedan ($975) with Red Seal Continental motor, V-shape radiator; five wire wheels; two-way hydraulic shock absorbers; four-wheel "steeldraulic" brakes; double drop frame; foot operated headlight dimmer. It carried a one year or 10,000 mile warranty.

The Durant firm, then a division of Dominion Motors, was making the Rugby truck.

FOSS

In 1897 George Foote Foss, Sherbrooke, Que., built one-cylinder, chain drive gas buggy. No reverse, tiller steering, water-cooled, racing sulky wheels. Engine started from driver's seat by a pull on leather strap; top speed, 12 mph (see also Chapter 1). Foss tried to sell in 1902; car backfired, knocked over prospective buyer, ripped his trousers and damaged his artificial leg. Eventually sold (to another man) for $75.

GALT

Canadian Motors Ltd., Galt, 1911-12; Galt Motor Co., 1913-15. First cars produced were Canada Tourist and Canada Roadster (see Canada). Then came the Galt in several models of roadster and five-passenger touring (prices $1475-$2350), 30-35 hp., 115" wheelbase, water-cooled, generator with storage battery and Connecticut distributor, multiple disc clutch, 4:1 gear ratio, 35 x 4" tires, combination force feed and gravity lubrication, I-beam front axle, full floating rear axle, Fowler semi-elliptic front springs; three-quarter scroll elliptic rear springs; fifteen gallon gas tank; royal blue with black trim; electric head, side and tail lamps; speedometer, electric horn. Galt also had electric starter: "The simple self-starting device is a boon to all, especially ladies, and does away with cranking by hand. It charges two of the cylinders with gas, compressing same ready for ignition."

However, the troublesome starter on 1912 models almost wiped out sales. Galt Motor Company in December 1913 received patent for storage-gas-electric model; production in 1914-15. A two-cylinder gasoline engine charged batteries which powered 600 rpm constant speed electric motor. Motor was geared 4:1 to rear axle through driveshaft and two universal joints. Could run 300 miles at 30 mph; battery took surplus energy on down-grades or at reduced speeds, giving it back at high speeds and on up-grades. Even when gasoline ran out, battery would carry car 15.2 miles.

GAREAU

Gareau Motor Co., Montreal, 1909-10. Touring body built by local carriage maker, four-cylinder engine of maker's design; only three believed to have been built. However as late as 1912 the firm was marketing the Amplex Valveless: "No valves and only nine working parts in the motor;" possibly a version of the U.S. Amplex.

GILSON

Gilson Manufacturing Co., Guelph, Ont. About 1920 this maker of farm equipment and gasoline engines made two touring cars. No commercial production.

GLEN

Scarborough Beach, Ont., 1922. About 1919 a Toronto engineer began work on this three-cylinder air-cooled cyclecar; straight line overhead valves; short crankshaft floated on two ball bearings and could be removed without disturbing engine; Rolls style radiator, cantilever springs, aluminum body, two-abreast seating, main members of steel tubular frame backed by cross-yokes; splash lubrication, cone clutch, 30 x 3½" tires, 102" wheelbase. Shown at 1922 Canadian National Exhibition.

GLOVER

In 1908 William Reston Dobbie of Pincher Creek, Alta., invested $8,000 in motor vehicle parts bought in Chicago, which he assembled at home and called a Glover. (Standard motor encyclopedias record no such car for U.S. although Glovers were sold later in England.) Long rangy vehicle resembled wagon with steps leading up the back, right-hand drive, crank in front, big buggy wheels and a fifth chain-driven wheel at the back, to be lowered to dig the car out when stuck. In practice the fifth wheel simply dug a deeper hole. Car was finally shipped to Winnipeg for an exhibition; then disappeared.

GRAMM

Gramm Motor Truck Co., Walkerville, Ont., 1913. This prominent (in its time) truck firm made a few two-cylinder air-cooled cyclecars with tandem seating, wood frame and belt drive.

GRAY

More in the novelty class but worth noting for ingenuity: Chatham's William Gray, of the family of Gray-Dort fame, built his own vehicle in 1905. It featured a steam engine-turned-gasoline engine on the back of a buggy, wheels driven by belts and pulleys. "I was able to place a belt tightener in such a position that I could slack off the belt and bring it to a stop," remembers Gray. "I had no gears or variation of speed at all. I applied a brake shoe to the steel-tired rim and by placing a cable and winch at the front was able to swing the axle of a regular buggy. Which, of course, in itself was extremely dangerous because if you hit one wheel with a jerk away it would go sideways. But it would run about 6 or 7 mph and we had a lot of fun with it on the main streets."

GRAY-DORT

Gray-Dort Motors Ltd., Chatham, Ont. 1915-25 (See also Chapter 6). Firm of carriage and sleigh makers (William Gray-Sons-Campbell Limited) associated with U.S. Dort. True production with Canadian-made components began in 1916. Over the years: several sports and touring models, from 1918 on having the famous four-cylinder Lycoming motor.

The Lycoming Model K, for example, had bore and stroke of $3\frac{1}{2}$ x 5", giving it about 192.4 cubic inch displacement. Crankshaft weighed 50 lbs. and together with a flywheel of about 50 lbs., Gray-Dort had considerable pulling power at low speeds; reached maximum torque around 1200/1500 rpm. Cast iron pistons with three rings; connecting rods were "I" forgings with a $\frac{7}{8}$" phosphorous bronze bushing at the top. Bearings over 2" wide. Lubrication was "pump and splash": bottom bearing-cap dipped oil from troughs (fed by tubes and a pump driven by an eccentric from the camshaft). Rapid turning of crankshaft actually created a mist, effectively oiling cylinder walls.

Side-draft Carter carburetor supplied gas to double exhaust manifold. Connecticut ignition had timer driven by a shaft whose gear meshed with another on the cam shaft.

Gray-Dort was a quality car in all respects. A 1917 model was upholstered with "genteel Narcissus cloth over deep soft cushions, the rich carpeting of Moresque wool, with various dainty appointments to add to its charm," but was "a man's car too."

The 1918 Gray-Dort sold for $945; had three forward speeds and reverse, internal expanding and external contracting brakes, elliptic front springs and full cantilever rear springs, emergency brake on the right pedal, service brake on the clutch pedal, linoleum-covered running board, 30 x 3½" Dominion tires, dashlight, ammeter, robe rail, foot rail, and a lock on the ignition switch. Special touring models in 1918 were in colors, mostly maroon, or green, often with tan top and yellow or natural wood wheels. One had a cigar lighter, and a combination dash and trouble light. Wire wheels were optional. In all early Gray-Dorts gas tank filler was on the instrument panel. By 1919 salesmen could sell all that the company produced (lifetime production: about 26,000). Costs fluctuated widely: 1919 touring car was $1275, a 1921 sedan, $3,000.

The 1921 Model 17 changed from traditional rounded radiator to a Rolls-Royce look; wheelbase lengthened to 108". By the end of 1922 more than 5,000 Gray-Dorts were registered in prairie provinces alone, ahead of Dodge, Maxwell and Studebaker. The 1923 four-cylinder touring model sold for $1095. Gray-Dort in its last year abandoned the four-cylinder model, which its followers considered a grave error. Meanwhile the U.S. Dort went out of business and Gray-Dort had to follow suit.

GUY

Matthew Guy Carriage and Automobile Co., Oshawa, 1910-11. Former Torontonian Guy got off to a shaky start in 1908 when Oshawa council voted him a $3,000 bonus to set up a factory to build hearses, in a former farm machinery works. Just as his project got started, the building collapsed. Two years later with capitalization of $250,000 he formed his carriage and auto firm to build the Guy 30, "a first class automobile." Produced a few 30 hp. touring cars and a one-ton truck.

HAMBRECHT

In 1907 Herman Hambrecht, Berlin (Kitchener), built a car similar to 1903 Cadillac; chain drive, rear-mounted engine, water and gas tanks in front; two speeds forward, reverse also served as brake. Hambrecht later worked for McLaughlin, then Kennedy Company of Preston, and quit the auto business in 1923.

IMP

Holden-Morgan Company Ltd., Toronto, 1913. This firm was incorporated in 1910 as "machinists, manufacturers, engineers and general contractors." Its two-cylinder cyclecar had a steel tube frame, aluminum body, 28" motorcycle wheels and seated one passenger behind the other.

This vehicle may have been related to the 1913 Imp produced by the W. H. McIntyre Co., of Auburn, Indiana.

The latter was also a two-cylinder cyclecar, air-cooled, V-type engine of 10-12 hp., belt drive to rear wheels, friction disc transmission, 100" wheelbase; two semi-elliptic springs at both front and rear mounted crosswise and some distance apart; vehicle frame was hung from the centres of the springs and outer ends of springs were connected to the steering knuckles; hence the Imp had no axles. Hood was five feet long. Brakes were wooden blocks applied to the driven pulleys on the rear wheels. Motor was started from front seat by means of a cable with handle attached to it (somewhat like an outboard motor). Overall weight: 450 lbs. Speed: 45 mph.

IROQUOIS

In July, 1906, promoter John F. Mills of Buffalo bought two acres of land in Welland, Ont.; subsequently set up Iroquois Motor Car Manufacturing Co. of Canada with $96,000 capitalization and including six Welland shareholders. Proposed to build 100 cars in first year with U.S. parts: 30 hp. and 40 hp. five-passenger models and a four-cylinder two-passenger 15 hp. runabout. By October, however, work had stopped, men were laid off and Mills was away "making arrangements for the purchase of machinery." Probably no significant production. May have been patterned on the Iroquois made in New York state during 1904-08.

IVANHOE

Canada Cycle and Motor Company, Toronto, 1903. Electric was designed by Hiram Percy Maxim, with battery weight balanced evenly over front and rear wheels (said to be a Canadian innovation); Westinghouse motor; could go 40 miles on one charge; 30" wheels; chain drive.

JULES 30

Jules Motor Car Co. Ltd., Guelph, 1911-12. Firm originally grew out of C. M. Preston company of Toronto which hired engineer Julius Haltenberger (hence "Jules") to build prototypes. Haltenberger and his staff had experience in France and Belgium. Preston sold to the newly incorporated Jules Motor Co. of Toronto, in late 1910, for $100,000. The plan to manufacture in Toronto then switched to Guelph, where arrangements were made with the old Morlock factory on Suffolk Street. The Jules, touted as the only totally Canadian car at that time, planned to have a five-passenger torpedo model, a four-passenger close-coupled torpedo, a roadster, coupe and the "Royal Torpedo" four-passenger car with detachable

double rear seat which could be turned into a semi-truck.

It claimed less than 500 parts, against 1700 or so for other contemporary cars. One novelty feature was an emergency brake foot pedal (which eliminated "at least ten parts") and a standard brake operating off the clutch pedal, so driver could brake with both feet and grasp the wheel with both hands. The horn button was reportedly in the middle of one brake pedal.

The Jules was made in six individual units: front axle and wheels, rear axle and wheels, steering, frame, body and motor, transmission and controls. It had four-cylinder cast-en-bloc 4 x 4½" 30 hp. motor; force feed constant level splash lubrication with sight dash inspection glass; multiple disc clutch; selective type three speed transmission and one reverse; Thermo syphon cooling system with vertical tube radiator; 18" steering wheel with spark and throttle levers on quadrant; pressed steel frame with 4¼" channel section, double set of internal expanding brakes operating directly on rear wheels, semi-elliptic front springs and patented flat design rear springs; I-beam section front axle and semi-floating-type rear axle; Bosch magneto; gravity feed carburetor; 112" wheelbase; 34 x 3½" wheels; 1950 lbs. overall weight; 10½" clearance; left-hand drive, $1500. By 1911 had two cars on the street and others reportedly in the making but total production unknown.

KEETON

Keeton Motors Ltd., Brantford, Ont., 1912-15. Reportedly a French-American make, adapted for Canadian roads and made in Brantford. Earliest model was six-cylinder, 48 hp. In 1914 and 1915 Keeton became a 35 hp., four-cylinder, five-passenger touring car with Northway power plant, Delco starting, lighting and ignition, Salisbury axles (rear axle floating with Hyatt roller bearings), V-shape radiator, wire wheels, left-hand drive, leather upholstery with mohair top; $1,390.

KELLY STEAM BUGGY

In 1884, twenty-five-year-old John Basil Kelly of Blyth, Ont., built a steam buggy after taking correspondence courses in steam and electrical engineering, and studying a threshing-machine traction engine. His two-passenger vehicle had lever steering, four artillery wheels with wooden spokes and iron tires, a second-hand Doty engine in front and a kerosene-fueled steam boiler under the seat. Chain drive led to a countershaft, connected to a sprocket on each rear wheel.

Kelly drove the buggy around Blyth, then dismantled it after people scoffed and horses jumped fences at sight of it.

Only his father, a flour and lumber miller, encouraged him. "Some day," predicted Kelly Sr., "men will drive machines like this and maybe even fly!"

KENNEDY

Kennedy Motor Co. Ltd., factory in Preston, Ont., head office in Galt; 1909-11. Shaft drive, 36″ and 38″ artillery-type wheels with solid rubber tires on earlier models; 30″ wheels with pneumatic tires on later models; 16-18 hp.; water cooled; speeds up to 25 mph; magneto and dry battery, Weston-Mott axles, Schebler carburetor, two or four passenger models, 90″ wheelbase, oil lamps; $750-$900. Advertisements stressed "The keen Kennedy is an automobile, not a motor carriage." Total production: about 175.

LAVOIE

Lavoie Automotive Devices Ltd., Montreal, 1923. Closed car, planned to be all-steel except portions of roof and corner pillars. Five-passenger sedan weighed only 2300 lbs; $1800. Also planned a Sedanon (coach-style body, $1900) and Sedanette (two- or three-passenger model with extra seat that folded into rear deck, $1950). Four-cylinder $3\frac{3}{8}$ x 5″ engine, 178.9 cu. in., cast with cylinders and upper crankcase in one piece, unjacketed detachable head. Water cooled; magneto ignition; multiple disc type clutch; three speeds forward and one reverse; 32 x 4″ tires; windshield wiper, rear view mirror, cigar lighter, two headlights, stop light, front and rear bumpers. Tail lamp and stop light were sunk in body panel to prevent breakage. Full elliptic-type springs, $39\frac{1}{2}$″ overall. All accessory controls on instrument board; all electric switches on steering column below wheel; horn button could be reached with a finger without moving hand from wheel. Interior trim to the belt line was leather, above that was painted; doors extended almost to top surface of running boards. The Lavoie had 116″ wheelbase and novel four-wheel brakes: internal expanding type designed to give uniform wear over entire contact area—nearly 360° of the drum circumference. Wheels and brakes were interchangeable and latter could be operated simultaneously by hand or foot. Unusually durable steering gear of screw and nut type. The Lavoie was so impressive that it rated eight pages in a U.S. motoring magazine. But it was short lived—probably too good for its time.

LEADER

The Leader Manufacturing Co., Toronto, 1901; listed as makers of bicycles and automobiles. By 1902, however, proprietors Silas and John Van Camp were running a lamp company, as was the third partner, William C. Hunt. Extent and nature of car production unknown.

LA MARNE

Anglo-American Motors Ltd., head office in Toronto, 1921. Designed and engineered in France by François Richard of Paris, who had previously built the Richard car in Cleveland. Anglo-American had Canadian patents for La Marne.

This firm produced at least one prototype, shown at 1921 Canadian National Exhibition: seven-passenger limousine with eight-cylinder-in-line Hispano-Suiza engine, aluminum body, tubular frame, 138" wheelbase, $3,000. Also planned the La Marne Junior, a four-passenger four-cylinder car, 116" wheelbase, $975. Plant to be located at Trenton, Ont., but in 1923 the company was reorganized and planned to build in La Prairie, Que.; evidently this plan also dissolved.

LEROY

Nelson Good and Dr. Milton Good, Berlin (Kitchener) 1899-1902. (*See* Chapter 2). One-cylinder, 4 hp. with overhead valves; water-cooled; flywheel weighed 64 pounds; 60" wheelbase; 28 x 3" pneumatic tires, overall weight, 950 lbs.

LOCOMOBILE

National Cycle and Automobile Company, Hamilton, 1902. Firm owned by B. H. Sills, an inventor of the cushion frame, Sills bumper and Sills Ritelite; then taken over by C.C.M. Assembled the Steam Locomobile, which undoubtedly resembled a U.S. car of that name: carriage body, two-cylinder engine, 14" boiler that had to be refilled every twenty miles, and tiller steering.

LONDON SIX

London Motors Ltd., London, Ont., 1921-25. Organized by William R. Stansell with $750,000 capital. Engine was six-cylinder L-head in-line Herschell-Spillman, 58 hp., mounted at an angle to use straight-through drive shaft and lessen wear on the universal. Aluminum body, over wooden frame made by Ingersoll casket maker; option of plain, painted or cloth-covered finish. Sedan, roadster, convertible and Canada's (maybe continent's) first hardtop which Stansell patented. Top speed: 70 mph. Standard equipment included eight-day Waltham clock, power tire pump and speedometer. A U.S. supplier wrote to the manufacturer, "Your car is a little too good. The London

Six is a far better car than the average owner appreciates until he drives one." About 98 cars produced; $2600-$3700. Stansell, in attempt to expand, ran out of funds.

MARITIME SINGER SIX

Maritime Motor Company Ltd., Saint John, N.B., 1913-14. Probably based on U.S. Singer. Variously advertised as 128″ and 134″ wheelbase; six-cylinder 50 hp. motor, C.R.G. three-jet carburetor, water-cooled, Westinghouse starting and lighting, multiple disc clutch, Firestone demountable-rim tires, 36″ wheels, Klaxon horn, left-hand drive, "shock preventers" on rear springs. Two- or five-passenger body, $3295; six-passenger, $3400; wire wheels, $100 extra. (*See* Dominion.)

MARTIN

Martin Carriage Works, Chatham, Ont. Occupied an old church building. Martin transmission was a large flat disc against which a small narrow wheel made contact. Moving this wheel back and forth from centre to circumference varied the speed of the vehicle, but the transmission was continually slipping. Four or five cars produced, early in the century.

MAXMOBILE

In 1900 D. A. Maxwell built a single three-passenger gas buggy in his Watford, Ont., blacksmith shop. He moulded the castings, did machining and woodwork, fitted rubber tires to 30″ buggy wheels. One-cylinder engine mounted under seat had 4″ bore and 6″ stroke, about 800 rpm's, pulled slowly but strongly up sharp grades. Transmission was two rubber belts running from engine to a short countershaft; two chains ran from countershaft to a huge sprocket fitted to sleeve slipped over rear axle. One drive wheel was connected to the sleeve. Two forward speeds, no reverse. Tiller steering; semi-elliptic springs; top speed, 20 mph; weight, 750 lbs. Radiator incorporated eighty ¾-inch brass tubes. Spray-type carburetor of his own design.

In 1910 Maxwell gave his machine a modern hood, pneumatic tires and a new floor to protect passengers from the machinery, since on one trip Mrs. Maxwell's skirt blew into the drive chains and was torn off. The car ran about twenty-four years.

McKAY

Nova Scotia Carriage Co., Kentville, N.S. and Nova Scotia Carriage and Motor Car Co., Amherst, N.S.; 1911-14. (*See* Chapter 2.) The McKay brothers' venture produced such cars as this typical Model 24 two-passenger torpedo roadster $1450): four-cylinder four-cycle 30 hp. long stroke motor, valved all on one side; pressed steel cone clutch, leather cased; sliding gear transmission, three forward and reverse; drop-forged beam section front axle, vanadium steel semi-floating rear axle; spoked wheels and 32 x 3½″ quick detachable tires; twenty-gallon gas tank; 17″ mahogany steering wheel; spark and throttle lever on top of wheel; foot accelerator on floor board; channel section frame of pressed nickel steel, 4 x 1½″; emergency and foot brakes; three-ply mahogany dash; dual high tension system Brigg's magneto, guaranteed for life; Model L Schebier carburetor; hand-buffed leather upholstery; self-starter (by late 1913 or early 1914); two gas headlamps, two oil side lamps, tail lamps, horn.

McLAUGHLIN-BUICK

(*See also* Chapter 3.) One of the earliest vehicles, Model F. sold for $1400 (top, $100 extra). Side entrance tonneau; five-passenger; 92″ wheelbase; 30 x 4″ tires; internal expanding brakes; pinion and sector steering, tilting column; three-quarters elliptic front springs, full elliptic rear; angle steel frame; double opposed 22 hp. motor; 4½ x 5″ cylinders; valves in cylinder head, cage and valve removable; water cooled; jump spark ignition, storage battery and dry cells in reserve. Mechanical force feed lubrication; Schebler carburetor; spark and throttle levers on top of wheel on immovable sector; foot pedals for slow speed ahead and reverse, side lever for engagement of clutch; planetary transmission, two speeds forward, one reverse; cone clutch; chain drive; fifteen-gallon gas tank; oil lamps, tail lamp, gas headlights, horn, repair outfit.

The Model 17 of calendar fame sold for $2150; five-passenger tonneau; 112″ wheelbase, 32 x 4″ tires; hub internal expansion brakes and external contraction on drive shaft; semi-elliptic front springs, full elliptic rear; 35-40 hp.; water-cooled; jump spark ignition; Schebler carburetor; cone clutch, sliding gear selective transmission, three forward, one reverse, shaft drive; deep cherry red.

MENARD AUTO BUGGY

Windsor Carriage and Wagon Works, Windsor, Ont., 1908-10. Moise L. "Mose" Menard, a native of Belle River, Ont., was a blacksmith-turned-wagon-maker who in 1910, at age 51, began building horseless carriages, designed by M. B. Covert of Detroit. The highwheeled auto buggy had a 4 x 4″ two-cylinder 16 hp. air-cooled motor set crosswise under the middle of the frame, hung low enough for full air circulation. An aluminum-faced

flywheel at the rear made contact with a friction wheel. Rear-wheel drive via $\frac{3}{8}''$ roller chains. A special clutch at each end of the countershaft equalized the driving wheel movement when turning. Wood and steel front axle, square-forged rear axle; three long full elliptic springs with radius rods to keep the axles in alignment. Sarven-type wheels, 36″, with 1¼″ solid rubber tires; 68″ wheelbase. Worm and sector gear steering. Spark and throttle controls under the wheel. Hand lever at the side moved the friction wheel to obtain different speeds. A ratchet pedal controlled the pressure of the friction wheel and a similar pedal operated the Raymond brake which acted on the countershaft. The reverse served as a brake for ordinary running. Typical buggy seat held two or three passengers. In 1910, facing stiff competition, particularly from Ford, Menard switched to truck making. In 1920 he sold to the Maple Leaf Manufacturing Company of Montreal.

MERCURY

Canadian Automobile Corporation, Lachine, Que., 1921. Started production of Mercury Six in mid-year, in former Rapid Tool and Machine plant. Seven Montreal directors, and an engineer and production expert formerly from Stevens-Duryea.

MOTTETTE

Canadian Motors Ltd., Toronto, 1900-03. President, J. T. Smith; manager, Alex Thompson. Operated on Yonge Street site of former Still Motor Company (*see* Still). Three-wheeled Mottette was one of the company's various electric vehicles, including a Tallyho bus. By 1904, C.C.M. occupied the site.

NEFF

Humberstone, Ont., 1899. Benton Neff, operator of a foundry in this village (since absorbed by Port Colborne, near Welland), turned from making steamboat engines to this two-passenger steam car. It had motorcycle-type wire wheels with Dunlop tires, an upright boiler, chain drive, bar steering and a brake on the rear axle. For emergency braking, could be put in reverse. Neff built only one, which was purchased decades later by Californian Nelson Holmwood, who planned to refurbish it and show it in Canada in 1970.

OXFORD

Oxford Motor Cars and Foundries Ltd., Montreal; 1913-15. Product of French Canadian industrialist family. Model A four-cylinder sold for $1600; Model C Six for $2950; touring cars. The Six was 48 hp.; 3¾″ x 5¼″; Bosch ignition, four speed transmission; dry plate multiple disc clutch; electric lighting and starting. Had sloping hood, low body line, folding tonneau seats, jiffy curtains. Nearly all components were imported. World War I cutback on supplies put firm out of business.

PARKER

Parker Motor Car Co. Ltd., Montreal, 1921-23. Closely resembled U.S. Birmingham. Built in former Forster plant; six-cylinder 70 hp. Red Seal Continental engine; seven-passenger touring, seven-passenger sedan and four-passenger sport model; Delco electrical system, Stromberg carburetor; 127″ wheelbase; Timken axles; 2½ x 7¾″ Z section frame with 38 x 2″ front and 58 x 2½″ rear semi-elliptic springs. Car originally announced as Royal Six; price "not to exceed $3,000." Dreams of 4,000 cars per year were never realized.

PECK

Peck Electric Ltd., Toronto, 1911-13; president, John Firstbrook, manager, Frederick George Peck. Firm was incorporated with $50,000 worth of machinery, plant and tools, for a host of activities including the buying, selling, leasing and manufacture of electric vehicles. Produced a coupe ($4000) available with chain or shaft drive and wheel or tiller steering; also roadster with chain drive and wheel steering. Slogan: "Keeps Pecking." Shown at 1912 Toronto Auto Show.

QUEEN

Queen City Cycle and Motor Works, Toronto, 1901. Only one car built; contemporary curved-dash Olds won the market. One-cylinder, chain drive, water-cooled, crank starter, one of first steering wheels in North America, wooden-spoke wheels, pneumatic tires. Two-passenger seating, with fold-down seat in front for two more.

REDPATH MESSENGER

Wooden body built in 1898 by Alfred Robinson of Toronto; chassis and running gear assembled in Kitchener-Guelph district. One-cylinder four-cycle engine; water-cooled block, remainder of engine air-cooled; updraught carburetor; water and gas both gravity-fed; right-hand steering; 2-speed transmission, forward and reverse; top speed, 10-12 mph.

REGAL

Regal Motor Co., Berlin (Kitchener), 1914-17. Organized by Henry Nyberg, who built Nyberg car in Indiana. First Regal produced May, 1915: four-cylinder Lycoming engine ($875) or V-8 ($1385); force-feed and splash lubrication; Atwater Kent unisparker; two headlights, tail light, Rushmore Regal direct system with dimmer attachment; pressed steel cone clutch; drive shaft mounted on two universal joints and enclosed in torsion tube; two sets of brakes operating on 12″ drums; rear axle three-quarter floating, geared at 3¾:1; front axle "I" beam drop-forged. Three speeds ahead and one reverse, 28 hp., 106″ wheelbase, 30 x 3½″ tires. Wartime shortage of materials squeezed this firm out of car business; Nyberg converted plant into Dominion Truck Company.

REGAL

A Regal also produced in Walkerville, Ont., about 1910; four-cylinder, four-cycle, 30 hp.; runabout, touring car, Baby Tonneau; three colors: brown, park lake and regal blue; wooden body; slogan: "The car that satisfies."

ROBERTS

Canadian Automobile Corp., Lachine, Que.; 1921. Several body styles; six-cylinder; announced at $4500-$5800 but may have built only one prototype. Probably related to Mercury Six.

ROSS

Ross Motor Car Company Ltd., Toronto, 1911-14, founded by car dealer William James Ross. In 1912 the firm displayed two "Canadian built cars"—a coupe and two-seat runabout—at the Toronto Auto Show. Although these may have been linked to a U.S. firm, the only American Ross models were a steamer (earlier) and a five-passenger gasoline vehicle in 1915. William Ross moved to Florida in 1914.

ROYAL

See Parker.

RUSSELL

Canada Cycle and Motor Co., (and C.C.M. subsidiary, Russell Motor Car Co. Limited) Toronto: 1905-15. (See also Chapter 2.) First car was five-passenger with detachable tonneau (hence convertible into runabout); wood frame, steel braced; elliptic rear springs; cross spring double-shackled in front; 30″ wheels; 3½″ tires; 12-14 hp.

4¾" bore and 4½" stroke horizontally opposed engine, 1,000 rpm's; shaft drive; water-cooled with cellular-type radiator; jump spark ignition from dashboard coil and batteries; 90" wheelbase; 1450 lbs weight. Throttle, spark and gear shift mounted on steering column; footbrake and emergency brake, both operating on rear wheels; ultramarine blue with black leather upholstery.

By 1908, there were four models, each available in touring or runabout, priced $1550-$4500. In 1909 Russell obtained exclusive Canadian rights for Knight sleeve valve engine. Before World War I this was one of most popular Canadian cars. Advertisements of 1915 offered Russell Light Six touring ($1475) and cabriolet ($1825) and Russell-Knight 32 four-cylinder, six and seven passenger ($2650 and $2750). Had branches in Hamilton, Montreal, Winnipeg, Calgary, Vancouver and Melbourne, Australia. Then went into war work; afterward plant acquired by Willys-Overland.

SAGER

United Motors Ltd., Welland, Ont., 1910-11. Firm was inspired by Frederick Sager of Detroit, formerly with the E.M.F. motor company and touted as "the pioneer automobile salesman in Canada ... intimately acquainted with practically every motor car agent and garage proprietor." Directors included Welland and Niagara Falls businessmen. Charter proposed to "buy, sell, trade in and carry on the business of manufacturing automobiles, cycles, bicycles, wagons, tricycles, motors, engines, carriages, delivery wagons, trucks, coaches, gasoline tractors, motor boats, biplanes, aeroplanes and dirigible air ships."

Sager planned to build a roadster and touring model (initially to be called the Welland) including "the best features of several cars," and reported the proposed 1911 production (300 cars) had been virtually sold out, sight unseen. Associated with Sager was Detroit engineer J. H. Gould, with previous experience in the U.S. Olds and Thomas automobile companies. The four-cylinder 30 hp. touring model sold for $1650. Extent of production unknown.

SHAMROCK

William Mimna, a Wardsville, Ont., stonecutter, tinkered at carmaking before the turn of the century. First known production was in 1904; one-cylinder gas buggy, belt drive, solid rear axle, clutch-and-belt system in lieu of gears. Radiator was a series of zigzag pipes with metal discs attached for radiation. Top speed was barely 10 mph and the car wouldn't climb hills.

Mimna built Shamrock II in 1914. On an early run he

drove astraddle a lounging cow, which rose, dumping car and passengers in a ditch. Mimna retired from auto business.

STILL

The Still Motor Co. Ltd., Toronto, 1899-1900. President, Thomas Bengough; mechanical engineer, W. J. Still (who helped design the Dickson-Fetherstonhaugh electric). Still built a 5 hp. *dos-a-dos* with 300 lb. air-cooled engine, wheel steering, wire wheels, 750 lbs. overall; $750. Firm has also been described as "Canadian Motor Syndicate" and "Canadian Electric Vehicle Co." It was apparently succeded by Canadian Motors Ltd. (*See* Mottette).

SUPERIOR

Petrolia, Ont., 1910. William English, wagon maker, produced about sixty open cars with steel body over wood frame, Atlas engine, planetary transmission; passenger version could be converted into a truck.

SWIFT

Chatham, Ont., early in the century, by the maker of the Anhut.

TATE

Tate Electrics Ltd., Windsor, 1912-13; coupe ($3600), roadster ($2700); wheel steering; also delivery vans of 500-1000 lb capacity and trucks of one, two, three and five-ton capacity. Co-directors were A. O. Tate and D. A. Dunlap, Toronto and Henry Timmins, N. A. Timmins, W. Scott Hutchinson, C. E. Archibold and S. Carsley, all of Montreal.

TAYLOR STEAM BUGGY

Henry Seth Taylor, Stanstead, Que., 1867. (*See also* Chapter 1.) Two-place open carriage; tiller steering, hooked to front wheels by rack and pinion mechanism; 3½" bore and 10" stroke; wood-fired steel boiler, 60 lbs pressure, containing 207 flues; vehicle weight, 500 pounds. Vehicle temporarily on loan to Ontario Institute of Science and Technology.

TUDHOPE

Tudhope Carriage Co. Ltd., and (from 1909) Tudhope Motor Company. (*See* Chapter 2.) First car about 1906 had two-cylinder air-cooled McIntyre engine from Indiana. Following the 1909 fire Tudhope turned to the four-cylinder 30 hp. U.S. Everitt, manufacturing body and all parts himself. When Everitt disbanded in 1911, Tudhope made cars under his own name, with a two-year guarantee. By 1913 electric starting and lights, spare tire, top and windshield were standard equipment; models: four-cylinder 36 hp. ($1625) and six-cylinder 48 hp. ($2500). In 1913 name changed to Fisher Motor Company; during the war both it and carriage company were devoted to war supplies. Tudhope stayed in the carriage business, also made some auto bodies, until 1924.

VICTORIAN

Two made, in vicinity of Hopewell, N.S., about 1896. Named after Queen Victoria. Two-cylinder two-passenger buggy with artillery wheels, iron tires, tiller steering, chain drive; cone-style clutch, one speed ahead, no reverse; no dashboard, top or lights. One now displayed in Niagara Falls antique car museum.

VINOT

Vinot Car Co. of Canada, Montreal, 1912-13. Incorporated as an affiliate of Vinot of France; had as subsidiaries the Fearless Tire Co. of Montreal and the Automobile Carriage Building Co. Directors included C. Ernest Gault, MLA, George Fairbanks, J. B. Ballargeon and J. E. Chapleau. J. A. Michaud was managing director.

At the 1912 Montreal Auto Show the firm exhibited a 35 hp. seven-passenger torpedo-type car; self starting; 60 mph with a full load. Repairs and overhaul were guaranteed for three years, but the manufacturer preferred "the purchaser to drive his own car as chauffeurs are reckless with good machines." This car was probably closely patterned on the French Vinot-Deguingand.

WALKER

In 1910 the Walker Motor Co., Walkerville, Ont. (C. M. Walker, chief stockholder) announced the Walker Six, a six-cylinder touring car and roadster with underslung frame. No evidence that Walker actually got into production.

WEL-DOER

Pollock-Welker Manufacturing Co., Berlin (Kitchener), 1912. Only one model of this two-cylinder cyclecar produced by inventors Alex H. Welker and Herman W. Doerr. A light open sports car designed to run fifty miles per gallon and up to 50 mph, slated to sell at $400. World War I killed further development.

WINDSOR
(*See* Dominion).

WINNIPEG
Winnipeg Motor Cars Ltd., Winnipeg, 1920-23. Opened first show room on Main one block south of Portage in early 1920, displaying touring, sport and sedan models with four-cylinder Herschell-Spillman engine. Slogan: "As Good as the Wheat." Frame and radiator made in Winnipeg. Radiator emblem had bright yellow sheaf of wheat tied with word "Winnipeg." Body colors predominantly dark green, dark blue, maroon. Company may have lasted four years and built as many as 500 cars at the plant near Winnipeg's Marion Bridge. One of the principals, L. M. Arsenault, evidently popped up later to produce cars in Saskatoon (*see* Derby).

WRIGHT
Montreal, 1929; Wright Flexible Axle touring car was based on Wright Fisher independent suspension system.

MAJOR U.S. MANUFACTURERS

Ford was the first, at Walkerville, Ont., in 1904 (*see* Chapter 4). General Motors' story is told in Chapter 3. For a time, Oldsmobile and then Reo made cars at St. Catharines. Around 1912 Schacht built cars and trucks in Hamilton; its 1912 Model J.M. was a 45-50 hp. touring car with self-starter and speedometer, known as "The Car with the Good Disposition." Hupp made the Hupmobile at Windsor. Fritchle Electric was made in Canada for eight years, and the Rollin was made here in 1924.

Willys-Overland took over Toronto's Russell in 1916, to make and sell Overland and Willys-Knight cars. Chalmers and Maxwell merged in 1917, and later became Chrysler of Canada. In 1921 W. C. Durant set up the Canadian arm of his new company in Leaside (then a Toronto suburb) to build Star, Durant and Flint Six cars.

Everitt-Metzger-Flanders (E.M.F.) moved in Walkerville in 1909; in 1913 it merged into Studebaker. In the thirties, Studebaker acquired Pierce-Arrow, Windsor becoming a distribution point for this luxury car. Packard assembled its first Windsor-made car in 1931; in 1954 was taken over by Studebaker. In the mid-twenties Dodge began assembling in a Toronto plant; about 1928, Chrysler took it over. Both Nash and Hudson began assembling in Canada in the thirties.

COMMERCIAL VEHICLES

Toronto's Canadian Motors Limited was possibly the first commercial vehicle maker, with an electric Tallyho bus in

1900. About the same time, CCM put together a fleet of Quadracycles, powered by de Dion-Bouton engines for the Toronto postal service. They were so low on power that the postmen sometimes had to back up steep hills.

Early in the century Chatham (Ont.) made a Denby truck and, briefly, a Symes Brothers stake truck. Before World War I the Russell car company made excellent two- and five-ton trucks. About the same time Redcliff Motors of Redcliff, Alta., near Medicine Hat, made trucks and buses. Petrolia, Clinton and Brantford trucks were all made in this period, in the Ontario towns of those names, while Ottawa's Watson Carriage Company made the Watson-Commerce.

After World War I truckmakers sprouted everywhere. A Veteran truck was produced briefly at Sherbrooke, Que. For a time there was a Graham plant in Toronto, Ruggles in London, Drednot in Montreal and Beaver in Hamilton. Also in Hamilton, the National Steel Car Co. Ltd., makers of railway cars and equipment, turned out the National truck in the mid-twenties.

By far the most successful truck firm of that era was Gotfredson of Walkerville, Ont., an affiliate of a Michigan firm, which outlasted and outproduced its parent. In its peak year Gotfredson manufactured 2,000 units; sold across Canada and in England.

Orillia, meanwhile, had a Yellow Cab Manufacturing Co., for export to England. Brooks of Stratford, Ont., made a few steam taxis and buses as well as cars. In Digby, N.S., the Defiant (later Warne) truck makers served the logging industry in the late twenties and early thirties. In Vancouver, Hayes-Anderson (later Hayes) started up in 1928 to make B.C. logging vehicles. By the thirties, Pacific Truck and Trailer Ltd., another Vancouver firm, was in business.

Quebec's Sicard Ltd., in business since 1927, started as a snow-plough maker and expanded into trucks.

THE SAD SHORT LIFE OF CALGARY CAR

In retrospect, say Calgary old-timers, the Calgary Car Company was ten years ahead of its time. That being so, it deserves a nod, if only as an example of the misery that could dog any motoring enterprise early in this century.

In 1907 the new company imported three buses from England, to run from the CPR station to Victoria Park, then east and north to the RCMP barracks. Significantly, the cars arrived on April Fool's Day. The fares were comparatively high, the distance relatively short and the service, to put it kindly, was less than perfect. Like most Canadian streets of the time, Calgary's were almost impassible in wet or snowy weather. The buses regularly sank in a slough near the police barracks, and as regularly were ignominiously hauled out by horse teams from the Pacific Cartage Co.

Customers wanted no part of this. Calgary Car's wretched four-month life is eloquently recorded in the diary of one R. Randolph Bruce, whose role with the firm is unstated, which is probably the way he preferred it.

April 6, 1907—The cars made their initial trip today, taking out the town council. One got stuck at the brewery flat.

April 8—Got the cars started running today.

May 6—Spent the morning at the car barn and the afternoon with Lott and Lineham. Things going badly. Decided to make a change.

May 7—Afternoon at Lott's office with Haggard whom we decided to try as manager of the car co.

May 29—Lineham, Lott and self spent afternoon discussing Calgary Car Co. Replaced Haggard with Healy.

Aug. 5—To settle Calgary Car Co.

Aug. 8—Spent part of the day with the cars. Lineham came in at night. Cars out of business so we could not take a run in them.

Aug. 9—Cars all in the barn today. Notified the man that the Calgary Car Co. had gone out of business.

Sept. 18—Went to car barn and saw cars. Very bad with rust.

HOW THE HORSELESS GREW AND GREW

Year	Passenger Vehicles	Commercial Vehicles
1903	178	
1910	5,890	
1915	60,688	533
1920	251,945	22,310
1925	641,186	74,938
1930	1,061,500	161,562
1935	992,114	173,518
1940	1,236,492	250,958
1945	1,161,337	321,550
1950	1,913,355	643,244
1955	2,960,874	951,525
1960	4,104,415	1,117,450
1965	5,279,373	1,345,438
1968	6,159,573	1,548,603

BIBLIOGRAPHY

Like all bibliographies, the one that follows is a faceless thing, with little indication of the scores of people and organizations that helped me find the pieces of this historical puzzle. I'm particularly indebted to Peter Weatherhead, Max Macdonald, Col. R. S. McLaughlin, Bill McCurdy, Dick Draper, Pat Curran, Norman C. Schneider, William Gray, Charlie Whipp and Herman Smith. I'm grateful, also, to the librarians and archivists of the Glenbow Museum in Calgary; Toronto, Hamilton, Buffalo, Detroit and Moose Jaw public libraries; the Saskatchewan, British Columbia and Prince Edward Island archives; the *London Free Press, Toronto Telegram, Hamilton Spectator, Winnipeg Tribune, Windsor Star, Montreal Star* and *Kitchener-Waterloo Record* libraries.

And most of all I thank Jane Sisson for listening, encouraging and making it all worthwhile.

CHAPTER 1:
Antique and Classic Car Club of Canada archives
Atlantic Advocate, October, 1957
Canadian Good Roads Association archives
Canadian Magazine, 1903, 1904, 1905
City of Belleville History, (W. C. Mikel, Picton Gazette Publishing Co.)
Isobel Eaglesham, Saskatchewan History and Folklore Society
Farmer's Advocate, January 30, 1908
General Motors Digest, 1949
Hamilton Automobile Club
Hamilton Spectator, April, 1908
History of the Alberta Motor Association, (Cashman)
Kitchener-Waterloo Record archives
Manitoba Motor League
Motoring Magazine of Canada, January, 1908
Motor Travel Magazine, 1916
Nova Scotia archives
Nova Scotia Department of Highways
Ontario Department of Highways
Ontario Motor League
Ottawa Journal, February 10, 1940
Prince Edward Island public archives
Quebec Automobile Club
Royal Automobile Club of Canada, Montreal
Saskatchewan *Hansard*, April, 1906
Statutes of Saskatchewan, 1906
Story of Canadian Roads, The, (E. C. Guillet, University of Toronto Press)
Toronto Telegram, June, 1923; July 22, 1927; July 8, 1963
Mrs. Victor Vallance, Burlington, Ont.
Vancouver Sunday Province, December 25, 1927
Wasaga Beach Weekly, August 4, 1950
Weekend Magazine, December 30, 1960
Winnipeg Telegram, May, 1908
Yours for the Driving, (Ford Motor Company)

CHAPTER 2:
Business Magazine, The, October, 1905
Doon, Ont., museum
DuPont of Canada automobile series
Encyclopedia of Motorcars, (Dutton)
Kitchener-Waterloo Record archives
LeRoy automobile handbook
Ken Liddell, *Calgary Herald*
London Free Press archives
Ontario Motor League
Ontario Motor League road book, 1912
Orillia Packet and Times, September 3, 1966
Norman C. Schneider, Kitchener
Timetable of Progress in Auto Safety, (Ward's Quarterly)

CHAPTER 3:
General Motors of Canada
Eric Hutton, *Maclean's Magazine*, September 15/October 15, 1954
Col. R. S. McLaughlin
Wheels For a Nation, (Frank Donovan, Crowell)

CHAPTER 4:
Elford Bell, Shamrock, Sask.
Big Change, The, (F. L. Allen, Harper & Bros.)
Canadian Motorist, (Ontario Motor League), 1913-20
Timothy C. Eaton, Toronto
Ford Times, Canadian Edition, 1913-16
Henry's Wonderful Model T, (Floyd Clymer, McGraw-Hill)
Motoring Magazine of Canada, 1908
Power to Go, The, (Merrill Denison, Doubleday)
Herman Smith, Ford of Canada, Oakville, Ont.
Story of the Ford in Canada, The, 1914 edition
Wheels For a Nation, (Frank Donovan, Crowell)

CHAPTER 5:
Canadian Good Roads Association
Canadian Motorist, (Ontario Motor League), 1914-20
History of the Alberta Motor Association, (Cashman)
London Free Press, July 1, 1967
Motoring Magazine of Canada, 1912
Nor-West Farmer, 1918
Regina Leader Post, 1910, 1911, 1914
Royal Automobile Club of Canada, Montreal
Saskatchewan archives
Story of Canadian Roads, The, (E. C. Guillet, University of Toronto Press)
Toronto Globe, February, 1913
Truckways (International Trucks brochure)

CHAPTER 6:
Antique and Classic Car Club of Canada archives
Canadian Motorist, (Ontario Motor League), 1914-20
Departments of Highways across Canada

Encyclopedia Britannica
Encyclopedia Canadiana
History of the Alberta Motor Association, (Cashman)
Imperial Oil Review, April, 1961
Petroleum Today (American Petroleum Institute)
Public Archives of Canada, Ottawa
Saskatoon Star, May 29, 1923
Tastemakers, The, (Russell Lynes, Harper & Bros.)
Toronto Globe, August 27, 1927
Wheels For a Nation, (Frank Donovan, Crowell)
Winnipeg Free Press, May 4, 1968

CHAPTER 7:
Canadian Good Roads Association
Gordon Doolittle, Toronto
Hamilton Motor Club
Imperial Oil Review, October, 1930; August, 1965
Memoirs of Frank Wood, Toronto
Ontario Motor League
Royal Automobile Club of Canada, Montreal

CHAPTER 8:
Automotive Industries, July 1, 1968
Canadian Petroleum, December, 1967
Canadian University, July/August, 1967
City of Toronto traffic engineering department
Dominion Bureau of Statistics
Ford of Canada
Globe Magazine, The, June 21, 1969
Imperial Oil Review, August, 1966
Metropolitan Toronto Police Department
Motor Vehicle Manufacturers Association
Ontario Department of Transport, 1968 road workshop
Ontario Motor League
These Canadians (N. K. Dhalla, McGraw-Hill)
Toronto Globe & Mail, November 13, 1968
Toronto Star, March 11, 1969

CHAPTER 9:
Antique and Classic Car Club of Canada archives
Canadian Motorist, (Ontario Motor League), August/September, 1960
Globe Magazine, The, October 20, 1962
Bill McCurdy, Halifax
Harley Neilson, Toronto
Herman Smith, Ford of Canada, Oakville, Ont.
Toronto Star, September 28, 1968
Toronto Telegram, October 7, 1967
Peter Weatherhead, Toronto
C. F. Wheaton, Saskatoon

CHAPTER 10:
Horst Kroll, Toronto

CHAPTER 11:
Atlantic Monthly, The, July, 1965
Canadian, The, January 25, 1969
Ford of Canada
General Motors of Canada
New York Magazine, February 24, 1969
Popular Science, December, 1968

Profiles of the Future, (Arthur C. Clarke, Harper and Row)
Reader's Digest, April, 1967
Science Journal, October, 1967
Toronto Globe & Mail, September 10, 1968; January 22, 1969
Wheels For a Nation, (Frank Donovan, Crowell)

THE CANADIAN CAR DIRECTORY:

Keith Acres, Ingleside, Ont.
Amherstburg Echo, May 3, August 30, 1912; May 27, August 5, 1921
Antique and Classic Car Club of Canada archives
Antique Auto Museum, Niagara Falls
Automobile, The, January 1, 15, 22, 1914; January 7, 1915
Automobile Topics, January 18, December 27, 1913; July 4, 1914; August 4, 1921
Automotive Industries, February 5, September 9, 1920
Canadian Automotive Museum, Oshawa
Harold Cooper, *Barrie Examiner*
L. H. Davis, Toronto
Fort Malden Museum, Amherstburg
Glenbow Museum, Calgary
William Gray, Chatham
Hamilton Spectator, October 15, 29, 1910; February 17, 1911
Historic Sketches of Oshawa, (T. E. Kaiser)
Nelson Holmwood, Laguna Beach, California
Horseless Age, August 17, 1910; September 3, 1913
A. J. Kendrick, Gilson Manufacturing Co., Guelph, Ont.
Kingston Whig-Standard, July 11, 1969
Jack Marins, Winnipeg Antique Car Club
Montreal Star, February 6, February 8, 1912
Moose Jaw Times Herald
Motor, February, 1907
Motor Age, January 18, 1912; August 11, September 1, 1921
Motor World, January 6, November 3, 1910; January 26, 1911; February 29, 1912
Ontario Government incorporation records for the makers of the Bell, Brock, Canadian, Clinton, Falcon, Guy, Imp, Jules, Keeton, London Six, Peck, Republic, Sager, Tate
Ontario Reformer, Oshawa, December 16, 1910
People's Press, Welland, August 16, October 4, December 20, 1910; January 24, 1911
Toronto City Directory, 1900-15
Toronto Globe, August 29, 31, 1910; September 7, 1911; February 24, February 26, September 7, 1912; February 24, August 23, 1913; February 18, 1914; August 26, 1916; August 25, 1917; August 27, 1921; August 26, 1922
Toronto Mail and Empire, May 16, 1929
Welland Telegraph, July 19, October 4, 1906; August 30, 1921
Welland Tribune, August 25, September 29, 1910
Charles Whipp, Petrolia, Ont.
Windsor Star, June 5, 1954; September 3, 1968

INDEX

Each Canadian car is listed in *The Canadian Car Directory*, pages 120 seq. Cars listed here in italics are those mentioned specifically in the text.

ACME 28
Alberni, B.C. 59
Alberta 64, 67, 70, 81, 85
Alberta Motor Association 77
Alberton, P.E.I. 12
American Motors 40
Amherst, N.S. 26, 57
Andrews, Dr. F. W. 49
Antique and Classic Car Club of Canada 98, 104
Apperson vii
Assiniboia, Sask. 7
Auburn 77, 104, 106
Auto Routes (Quebec) 85

BALLANTYNE, Dr. C. T. 51
Banff 63
Barrie, Ont. 27
Bartlett 23
Belcourt, Rev. Georges 2
Bell, Elford 50
Belleville, Ont. 6
Bennett buggy 78
Bennett, Richard Bedford 78
Bentley 93
Blind River 58
Bosch (Canada) 111
Bouladon, Gabriel 116, 118
Boulding, Kenneth 89
Bourassa, H. E. 20
Bourassa Six vii, 73
British Columbia 11, 23, 64, 71, 81, 115
British Petroleum, Ltd. 111
Brockville, Ont. 33
Brooks, Oland J. 76, 77
Brooks Steamer 75, 77
Buick 26, 36, 37, 39, 41, 42, 43
Buick (engine) 38
Burlington, Ont. 1

CADILLAC 5, 37, 39, 73, 93, 96, 103, 105
Calder, Sheriff 53
Calgary 4, 53, 62, 63, 67, 68, 71, 113, 115
Campbell, Dr. G. D. 94
Campbell, John 103
Canada Cycle and Motor Company (CCM) 23, 24, 25
Canadian Automobile Association 82
Canadian Baby Car 21
Canadian Good Roads Association (CGRA), 60, 71, 81, 82, 84, 94
Canadian Highways Act (1919) 82

Canadian Queen, see *Queen*
Cappon, Dr. Daniel 92
Carstairs, Alta. 68
Castlegar, B.C. 58
Champion Spark Plug Company 39
Chandler 77
Charlottetown, P.E.I. 12
Chatham 28
Chatham, Ont. 23, 74, 75
Chevrolet 37, 41, 42, 55, 84, 93, 99, 103
Chevrolet, Arthur 40
Chevrolet (engine) 107
Chevrolet, Louie 39, 40
Chrysler, 37, 74, 106, 118
Chrysler, Walter 37, 39
Clarke, Arthur C. 114
Classic Car Register 97
Cobalt 84
Cochrane, W. F. "Billy" 4
Comet 25, 28
Concord (carriage body) 34
Conover, Frederick 55
Cord, 77, 104
Corinne, Sask. 53
Corvette 93
Cougar 93
Couzens, James 46
Creston, B. C. 58, 79
Crow 21
Crowsnest Pass, 58
Currie, A. 94
Curry, John 46

DALI, SALVADOR 99
Dallegret, François 99
Dandurand, Henri 60, 75, 76
Dandurand, U. H. 3
Davis 21
Dawson City, 53
Derby 73
Dickinson, George "Sneaky Dick" 66
Dietrich, (body) 96
Ditmars, W. C. 4
Dodge 74
Dodington, Paul 105
Dominion Bureau of Statistics 89, 91
Doolittle Demountable Rim 83, 86
Doolittle, Dr. Perry Ernest 13, 14, 79, 80, 82, 83, 84, 85, 86
Doon, Ont. 19
Dort, Josiah 75
Dort (U.S.) 74
Drumheller, Alta. 68
Drummondville, Que. 51
Duesenberg 77, 104
Dunlop Canada, Ltd. 16, 23, 78
Duplex 21, 73
Du Pont 39
Durant 74, 77

Durant Dort Carriage Company 40
Durant, William Crapo 36, 37, 38, 39, 40, 41, 74
Duryea, Charles E. and J. Frank vii, 3

EATON, GEORGE 109
Eaton, John Craig (later Sir John) 4, 64, 80
Eaton, Timothy 2, 4
Eaton, Timothy Craig 51
Edington, Gordon 103
Edmonton 52, 63, 64, 67, 71, 82, 113, 115
Emmett, A. C. "Ace" 5
Englestad, C. P. 53
Enniskillen, Ont. 31
Everitt 27

FAWCETT, RON 103, 105
Fetherstonhaugh, Frederick 3
Fiberglas Canada Ltd. 111
Firebird 108
Flickenger, Edward 84
Flying Cloud 72
Ford 9, 12, 35, 45, 46, 47, 74, 93, 117
Ford, Henry vii, 3, 14, 37, 40, 45, 46, 47, 54, 55
Ford, Model A #55
Ford, Model C #47, 106
Ford, Model T #44, 45, 47, 48, 49, 50, 51, 53, 54, 55, 96, 104, 105, 106
Ford Motor Company 40, 46, 118
Ford of Canada 46, 47, 50, 54, 55, 84, 106
Forster 73
Fort William 102
Foss, George Foote 3
Fossmobile vii
Franklin 77

GALT 21
Galt, Ont. 11, 51
General Electric (Schenectady) 116, 117
General Motors (U.S.) 39, 40, 41, 42, 74, 118
General Motors of Canada 30, 42
Gliddens, C. J. 62
Glover 22
Good, Dr. Milton 16, 17, 19
Good, Nelson 11, 16, 17, 19
Goodyear Rubber Company 52
Gorrie 12
Gray-Dort 23, 70, 74, 75, 77, 99
Gray, Robert 75
Ground Effect Machines 114
Grundy, C. F. 11
Guelph, Ont. 22
Gwin, Wilbur 78

HALIFAX, N.S. 26, 57, 59, 103, 104
Hambrecht, Herman 20
Hamilton, Ont. 1, 2, 11, 51, 75, 80, 99
Haney, F. V. 57, 59
Harewood, Ont. 111
Headingly, Man. 5
Hertz, P.B. 104
Hezzlewood, Oliver 35, 36
Hispano-Suiza (engine) 74
Hodgetts, Craig 118
Hops, B.C. 45
Hupmobile 77

IMPERIAL OIL 63, 86
Industrial Metal of Canada, Ltd. 94
Ingersoll, Ont. 21
Innisfail, Alta. 68
Iroquois 21
Iroquois Falls, 83
Ivanhoe 21, 23, 116

JACKSON 36, 37
Jarvis, S.D. 51
Jasper 63, 82
Joliette, Que. 7
Jordan 77
Jules 22

KANE, W. L. 10
Kelly-Porsche, see *Porsche*
Kennedy 28
Kentsville, N.S. 25
Kingston, Ont. 21, 25
Kiskinook, 79
Kissel 77
Kitchener, B.C. 58
Kitchener, Ont. 7, 16, 20
Knight (engine) 25
Kroll, Brigit 108, 112
Kroll, Hildegarde 108
Kroll, Horst 107, 108, 109, 110, 111, 112

LA MARNE 74
Lane, Robert 99
Laprarie Dyke, Que. 81
Latta, S. J. 82
Lavoie 73
Leaside, Ont. 74
Leduc, Alta. 68
Leroux, Ulric 51
LeRoy vii, 11, 16, 17, 18, 19
Lethbridge, 59
Lincoln 72, 93
Locomobile 4, 77
Loewy, Raymond 117, 118
Lola 107, 108, 110, 111
London Six 21, 75, 77
Lumsden, Sask. 60

MACREE, J. V. 15
McCurdy, Bill 104
Macdonald-Cartier Freeway 85

Macfarlane, Brigadier R. A. 80, 84
MacGillivray, Kenneth 80, 84
McGregor, Gordon 46, 47
McKay 26, 28, 104
McKay, Dan 25, 26
McKay, Jack 25, 26
McKay Stan 26
McLaren 109
McLaughlin-Buick 29, 39, 46, 60, 67, 68, 103, 104
McLaughlin Carriage Company 29, 34, 35, 38, 39
McLaughlin, Col. Robert Samuel 28, 30, 31, 33, 34, 35, 36, 37, 38, 39, 40, 41, 42, 43
McLaughlin, George 33, 35, 37, 41, 42
McLaughlin, John 33
McLaughlin, Robert ("The Governor") 31, 33, 34, 36, 37, 41, 42, 43
McLaurin, Dr. R. 60
McLeod, Dr. Norman 86
McLeod, Finlay 53
McLuhan, Marshall 92, 115
Mallory, F. R. 45
Manitoba 5, 70, 73, 80
Maple Lake, Ont. 103
Maritimes 23, 34, 71
Marmon 77
Maxmobile vii, 64
Maxwell 77, 104
Maxwell, Mrs. D. A. 64
Meggs, Charlie 53
Menard vii, 28
Mercedes-Benz 95
Metropolitan Toronto 87, 88, 92, 115
Metropolitan Toronto Police 87
Milbrath, Arthur 37, 38
Millen, George 5
Mimico, Ont. 13
Mimna, William 20
Model T, see Ford, Model T
Montreal 7, 20, 21, 25, 59, 60, 73, 80, 83, 99, 103, 113, 115
Moodie, John 1, 2, 4, 14
Moon 77
Moose Jaw, 59
Morriss, Joe 64
Morrison, W. H. 4
Mosport Racing Park 107, 108, 110
Moss, Sterling 93, 108
Mustang 93, 108
Myers, Court 99

NASH, CHARLES 40
Nash Motor Company 40
Neilson, Harley 95, 96, 97
Neville, Charles 104
New Brunswick 65, 80
Niagara Falls, Ont. 23, 97
North Bay 58
Nova Scotia 10, 11, 26, 65

OAKLAND 37, 39
Oakville, Ont. 13, 92
Oldfield, Barney 14, 15, 68
Olds, Ransom E. 19, 20, 39
Oldsmobile 19, 37, 39, 106
Ontario 11, 12, 34, 63, 64, 65, 66, 69, 71, 80, 98, 103, 104, 107, 110, 113
Ontario Department of Highways 91
Ontario Department of Transport 91
Ontario Humane Society 71
Ontario Motor League, The 66, 71, 83, 87, 92
Ontario Provincial Police 87
Orillia, Ont. 26, 27, 41, 102
Oshawa Automotive Museum 39
Oshawa, Ont. 30, 31, 34, 35, 36, 37, 41, 42, 92
Ottawa 5, 51, 59, 115
Overland 77

PACKARD 6, 55, 64, 71, 75, 95, 96, 97, 99
Packard-Darrin, see Packard
Packard-Dietrich, see Packard
Packard, Vance 92
Paige 77
Paris, Ont. 53
Parker 73
Pask, S. M. 104
Pease, Al 111
Peerless 14, 36, 77
Penn 25
Peterson, Oscar 14
Pierce-Arrow 36, 72, 77, 104
Pierce, Richard 36
Pincher Creek, Alta. 22
Playford, Steve 67
Pleva, Professor E. G. 85
Plymouth 37
Pogue, Charles N. 78
Pontiac 37
Porsche 109, 110
Port Hope, Ont. 45
Poplar Point, Man. 10

Portage La Prairie, Man. 10
Prince Edward Island 12, 25, 26, 73

QUEBEC 11, 25, 34, 64, 65, 69, 80, 81, 82, 83, 85
Quebec City 113
Queen 22, 103

REGINA 5, 46, 60
Reo 19, 36, 57, 77
Ribble, Ira 51
Ridgeway, Ont. 106
Rivard, L. C. 7
Robinson, Alvy, 51
Rolls-Royce 93, 95, 99, 102
Russell 23, 25, 28, 46
Russell-Knight, see Russell
Russell, Tommy 24, 39
Rustico, P.E.I. 2

SABROWSKI, WALTER 110, 111
St. Catharines 80
Saint John, N.B. 80
St. John's 85
St. Johns, Que. 80
St. Stephen, N.B. 80
Ste. Rose, Que. 80
Saskatchewan 11, 60, 69, 78, 82, 84
Saskatoon 53, 70, 73, 99, 102, 104
Sault Ste. Marie 58
Schultzhauer, Moses 16, 17, 18, 19
Sears 103
Shamrock, Sask. 50
Sherbrooke, Que. 3
Sloan, Alfred P. 39
Smith, Herman 106
Smith, W. S. 13
Spence's Bridge, 79
Stanhope (carriage body) 34
Stanley (brothers) 4
Stanley Steamer 75
Star 74
Stanstead, Que. 3
Stewart, Dr. P. J. 116
Still 115
Stratford, Ont. 16, 75, 76
Studebaker 72, 73, 74
Stutz Bearcat 72, 77
Summerland, B.C. 49
Swift Current 83

TAYLOR, HENRY SETH 3
Temagami 84

Thomas Flyer 36
Three Rivers, Que. 83
Todd Medal 80
Toronto 2, 10, 11, 13, 16, 22, 23, 25, 33, 41, 53, 58, 59, 66, 71, 75, 76, 78, 80, 83, 94, 95, 98, 99, 103, 104, 105, 109, 112, 116
Trail, B.C. 58
Trans-Canada Highway 84, 85
Trans-Canada Highway Act (1949) 84
Trenton, Ont. 74
Trumper 7
Trumper, Ben 7
Tudhope 27, 28, 103
Tudhope, J. B. 26, 27, 41
Tudhope-McIntyre, see Tudhope
Tudhope Motor Company 26, 27, 28

VANCOUVER, B. C. 4, 51, 59, 63, 79
Victoria, B.C. 85
Volkswagen of Canada 109

WALKER, LESTER 118
Walkerville Wagon Works 46, 47
Wallace, "Scotty" 59
Waltham 3, 75
Wardsville, Ont. 20
Watford, Ont. 64
Weatherhead, Peter 98, 99
Webb, Fred 70
Welch, Paul 67, 68, 69
Weyburn, Ont. 7
Wheaton, C. F. 99, 102
Whitby, Ont. 103
Wietzes, Eppie 112
Wilby, J. W. 57
Willys 74
Windsor, Ont. 45, 46, 75
Wingham, Ont. 53
Winnipeg 73
Winnipeg 5, 10, 11, 52, 53, 58, 62, 73, 78, 80, 83, 115
Winton 1, 2, 4, 13, 14, 64, 104
Wolseley 104
Wood, Frank 83
Woodstock 51
Wright 73

YAHK, B.C. 58
Yarmouth, N.S. 26
Yates, William "Dad" 45

KEETON, 1913 - BRANTFORD

RUSSELL, 1914 - TORONTO